T0220258

BROKEN AGILE

STORIES FROM THE TRENCHES

Second Edition

Tim Brizard

Apress®

Broken Agile: Stories from the Trenches

ISBN-13 (pbk): 978-1-4842-1744-3

ISBN-13 (electronic): 978-1-4842-1745-0

Trademarked names, logos, and images may appear in this book. Rather than use a trademark symbol with every occurrence of a trademarked name, logo, or image we use the names, logos, and images only in an editorial fashion and to the benefit of the trademark owner, with no intention of infringement of the trademark.

The use in this publication of trade names, trademarks, service marks, and similar terms, even if they are not identified as such, is not to be taken as an expression of opinion as to whether or not they are subject to proprietary rights.

While the advice and information in this book are believed to be true and accurate at the date of publication, neither the authors nor the editors nor the publisher can accept any legal responsibility for any errors or omissions that may be made. The publisher makes no warranty, express or implied, with respect to the material contained herein.

Managing Director: Welmoed Spahr
Lead Editor: Steve Anglin
Editorial Board: Steve Anglin, Louise Corrigan, Jonathan Gennick, Robert Hutchinson, Michelle Lowman, James Markham, Susan McDermott, Matthew Moodie, Jeffrey Pepper, Douglas Pundick, Ben Renow-Clarke, Gwenan Spearing
Coordinating Editor: Mark Powers
Copy Editor: Lori Jacobs
Compositor: SPi Global
Indexer: SPi Global
Artist: SPi Global

Distributed to the book trade worldwide by Springer Science+Business Media New York, 233 Spring Street, 6th Floor, New York, NY 10013. Phone 1-800-SPRINGER, fax (201) 348-4505, e-mail orders-ny@springer-sbm.com, or visit www.springeronline.com. Apress Media, LLC is a California LLC and the sole member (owner) is Springer Science + Business Media Finance Inc (SSBM Finance Inc). SSBM Finance Inc is a Delaware corporation.

For information on translations, please e-mail rights@apress.com, or visit www.apress.com.

Apress and friends of ED books may be purchased in bulk for academic, corporate, or promotional use. eBook versions and licenses are also available for most titles. For more information, reference our Special Bulk Sales–eBook Licensing web page at www.apress.com/bulk-sales.

Any source code or other supplementary materials referenced by the author in this text is available to readers at www.apress.com/9781484217443. For detailed information about how to locate your book's source code, go to www.apress.com/source-code/.

This book is dedicated to all the developers that work day in and day out to produce quality software that delivers value to the business and makes people's lives better. Your long hours, dedication to craft, and ability to get the job done despite all challenges is a source of inspiration.

Contents

About the Author

Tim Brizard is a software engineer in Orlando, Florida. He has designed and developed enterprise-level systems since 1997. His experience includes architecting solutions for small and large companies alike. He started his career using programming languages such as C, COBOL, and RPG. Later he started to use object-oriented languages such as C++ and Java. He has a comprehensive knowledge of object-oriented languages, distributed computing, and database solutions. His architecture experience ranges from simple client-server to n-tier applications. He has a passion for software delivery and teaching others about improving the quality of software.

Acknowledgments

My completion of this book could not have been accomplished without the support of all those that I have been fortunate enough to work with over the years. To my loving family and great friends, your help and thoughtful support were truly appreciated.

Introduction

I am going to begin with a few comments about the purpose of this book and what went into writing it.

The book is based on more than six years of working on several projects using Agile software development methodology. These projects began at several different companies, across several industries, and varied in size from small to extremely large.

This volume is a set of perspectives and stories from the trenches of these Agile projects based on my experiences as a senior software engineer, a technical lead, and an automation engineer.

It is as much a telling of what can go wrong using Agile as it is a guide on how to avoid land mines.

The purpose of the book is not to point out mistakes by management or others. Rather, it is told from the standpoint of people who had to deal with decisions made by managers and how better planning and understanding could have gone a long way. It is definitely an opinionated view, and I do not claim here to have all the answers. By sharing these stories and perspectives, ideally, some development teams may be spared the headaches and frustration that I've seen.

Here's a note about the format. Each chapter outlines a specific challenge and then provides some real-life stories that illustrate these challenges. However, these stories are not just about negative experiences. There are also some positive stories that demonstrate how the challenges were handled well. Finally, for each story I provide some advice on how to avoid the same pitfalls or, in the case of positive stories, point out what can be emulated.

This is not strictly a book on Agile software development. It talks more broadly about how management's decisions can really hurt morale, contribute to terrible code quality, and ultimately cause the best employees to seek opportunities elsewhere. While knowledge of Agile software development is not a requirement to read this book, it will make understanding some of the stories and terminology easier.

So, who should read this book? Well, our readers could be anyone who has been involved in Agile projects, or development projects in general, who would like to hear about what is happening in other companies, or anyone who is looking for some advice on how to improve the process of adopting Agile in his or her company. Finally, some developers may simply enjoy reading this book because they can relate to the stories.

Scale Success

Scaling is always a difficult challenge; whether it is in manufacturing, in growing a small business, or in software development. For organizations that are trying to adopt the Agile software development methodology, successfully scaling presents some unique challenges. Often scaling too quickly leads to problems that people blame on Agile. In reality, the problems could have been avoided, or at least mitigated, if more upfront planning had been done. This chapter looks at what can happen when an organization scales its Agile teams without learning from the success stories of other Agile teams.

Real-Life Stories

Story 1: Learn from the Success of Others

I was once part of an Agile project team that had only been using Scrum for about eight months or so when we were asked to start on a project with a very aggressive timeline. We tried several different approaches in the first month of the project, eventually deciding to use Kanban. We chose Kanban because the project was moving so fast and we needed to work in a "just-in-time" fashion. The project was to rewrite an existing application that took about a year and a half to build. We were able to rewrite the application in six months and deliver it to Production with no major defects.

Our team became very popular in the organization. People wanted to know how we worked: they asked questions like "how are you doing automated testing?" and "how do you manage Work In Progress Limits?" It was a great feeling to be part of a successful Agile team. We were selected to work on a new project that would be one of the biggest ever for the organization. This is where it got interesting.

Management split our team into several new teams. Instead of keeping the processes and things that made the team so productive, these new managers chose to start from scratch. I think this was mostly a case of managers who were new to Agile and wanted to try their own ideas of how to manage Agile teams. But the main issue was that for this project, they spun up about 20 teams. The members of these teams were more or less new to Agile. In this case, there were no Agile Coaches (either from internal employees who had Agile experience or from outside the company) and the teams tended to have a lot of problems. There was very little consistency across teams and everyone had to relearn the same pain points. This led to all kinds of issues for the project, including poor-quality software and a lot of people becoming burned out due to a lack of understanding of velocities and mandated Sprint commitments (yes, mandated, but I will discuss that later, in Chapter 7).

Thoughts

The project described above was extraordinary in many ways, including the number of Scrum teams that were formed in a short amount of time. But even with that being the case, there were still things that could have been done to set the teams up for success and not failure.

For instance, this organization had used Scrum for about two years on several prior projects. Most of this experience was concentrated in just a few teams, some of which, by all accounts, had been pretty successful. We could have seeded some of the new teams with members from the seasoned teams. We could have hired Agile Coaches to assist these new teams for the first few months. Management could have inquired about what had made the experienced teams successful on their past projects—which is important because these teams knew how to use Agile within their organization—and passed the information on. That is key because what works in one organization does not necessarily work in another.

Story 2: Share Knowledge Across Teams

I was fortunate to be a technical lead of a highly productive Scrum team on another large project with more than a dozen teams. We made great use of the Retrospective meeting at the end of the two-week Sprint. We used it to try new things to address pain points and were constantly improving. The team was not afraid to try a lot of new things (everything from how we wrote acceptance criteria in User Stories to the way developers collaborated with the Business Analyst and Quality Assurance engineer).

But an interesting thing happened when managers tried to get other teams to adopt some of our processes. These other Scrum teams were very resistant to change and there was a lot of pushback. Ultimately, the managers did not push the issue. The unfortunate part is that these other Scrum teams might have learned better ways to do things, but that sharing never happened.

Thoughts

I'm not saying that what works for one team will necessarily work for another team. But when something is proven to work really well for one team, why not try to spread it to other teams? Maybe other teams will try something new and in the Retrospective they decide that the change didn't work. They can always revert back to the way they were working before. This seems like a very natural way for an Agile team to operate. I see Agile teams as incubators, and when one team finds a better way to do something that leads to better-quality software, better collaboration, and improved velocity, then why not try to spread that knowledge to other teams.

Communication

What is the best way to foster an environment where development teams feel like they can talk about issues openly and developers feel like they are being kept in the loop? Furthermore, how do you ensure that the cross-functional team members on an Agile team are collaborating in a way that is productive? Finally, how do you make sure that "communication overload" does not happen (too many e-mails, etc.)? This is not always easy to achieve; it may be easy to talk about in concept, but making it work is a different story.

Real-Life Stories

Story 1: Lack of Transparency

I was on an Agile project that was using Kanban, and from a development point of view the project was very successful. However, in terms of communication from managers, it was not so successful. It was a multiphase project. As we approached the end of phase 1, we received very little communication about whether phase 2 would happen. Most of the developers on this project were "borrowed" from other teams, and it was uncertain where they would go back to or even if there was a team to go back to. Of course, this led to uncertainty and was not good for productivity.

Thoughts

One of the things I like most about Agile is the idea of transparency. Usually we think of transparency between the development team and the Product Owner, but I think transparency at every level is always a good thing. It's understandable that management does not want to communicate plans when they are not 100% solidified. But I feel that management should at least communicate something, even if that something is "we are still working out the details on XYZ." This shuts down any rumors and makes people feel they are being kept in the loop. This is definitely not an Agile-specific concern or unique to any one company. But I do think that for organizations adopting Agile, being more transparent provides an opportunity to improve overall communication.

Story 2: Leadership Frustration

Conversely, I was on a project where the manager shared too much. In the Daily Stand-up meeting, he would let us know that things were still being decided, which was good to hear, but the problem was that he showed his own frustration with the leadership above him and admitted to having very little confidence in those leaders.

Thoughts

I think this story shows the opposite end of the spectrum: that there needs to be a balance. It is good for managers to share what they know, but perhaps they shouldn't share every detail and perhaps they should wait until things are semisolidified. That way, team members feel they are being kept in the loop, but they don't have to deal with the yo-yo effect of things that change on a day-to-day basis.

Story 3: Bridging a Communication Gap

On one Scrum team we were having problems with writing clear acceptance criteria for User Stories. There was a disconnect between what the Product Owner, Quality Assurance (QA) engineer, and developer thought the User Story was about. I had just read the book *Specification by Example* by Gojko Adzic (Manning Books, 2011) and suggested we try the "three amigos" concept. This approach seemed to be a good fit because we had a lot of access to our Product Owner. So we had the developer, QA, and Business Analyst (BA) (a proxy for the Product Owner on this team) meet to talk through the User Story. This process worked incredibly well for this team. By the time the meeting was over, all three were on the same page and for the most part the acceptance criteria were fleshed out. After the meeting, the developer usually had enough information to implement the User Story and the QA engineer had enough information to finish writing the acceptance criteria.

Thoughts

The changes discussed in Story 3 improved communication between team members. In addition, because everyone was on the same page coming out of the meeting, it led to the team building the right software. Finally, the better the communication between members of a cross-functional team, the better the quality of the software will be and the more the team members will feel like a team working toward the same goal.

The changes in the team were incredibly noticeable. The changes led to a better velocity, and because we used the "three amigos" approach (i.e., we had the entire team in a single Story Time meeting), we wasted less time. I cannot overstate the importance of maximizing developers' time and having better communication between team members on an Agile team.

Story 4: Communication Breakdown

I was on yet another Scrum team where communication between team members was not very good. The Daily Stand-up meeting lacked focus. The team did the normal "around the room" process, but beyond that there was little control. It was very common to have side conversations going on, for people to go off on tangents, and even to have people skip the meeting. Sometimes the meetings were even cancelled because several team members could not attend. One consequence of this lack of structure was that some team members often didn't know what the other team members were working on.

Thoughts

One of the reasons for the Daily Stand-up meeting is to increase communication on a team. Having some amount of structure and asking the three questions (What did you do yesterday? What are you doing today? Are you blocked by anything?) are just guidelines, but for most teams they serve as a good starting point. The meeting should only take about 15 minutes. I've typically scheduled the Daily Stand-up for 30 minutes with the first 15 being what I just described and the last 15 being for post-Scrum items (things that the whole team cares about, or at least things that could benefit the team members if they heard the conversation). Anything that the whole team would not benefit from hearing should be taken offline.

The main goal is that people on the team should know what other team members are doing; thus they can swarm on things that are blocking someone. Skipping a meeting is a bad idea for a couple of reasons. First, just because some people cannot attend doesn't mean that the meeting won't have value for the rest of the team. Second, it breaks the cadence of the team, which can be detrimental.

Story 5: Lack of Productivity

While on a small e-commerce team (nine developers), I had to attend a daily 9 a.m. meeting. All developers had to attend this meeting. The problem was that usually the developers were working on completely different projects. After about a week of attending these meetings, I asked some other team members, "Do you find this useful?" The answer I received from all of them was a quick "no." Every day I noticed that most of the developers would bring their laptop into the meeting and would hardly pay attention to what was going on in the meeting, which lasted for about 30 minutes. I would like to say that there was some value to these meetings, but that was usually just not the case. However, the manager was insistent that everyone be there at 9 a.m. sharp. In one meeting I recall we spent almost the entire time watching the manager try to test a defect that had been discovered. Unfortunately, this manager didn't realize that the value of the meeting was basically nonexistent. I should mention that this team was moving toward Scrum but did not claim to be an Agile team.

Thoughts

I thought that Story 5 provided a good example of a missed opportunity for productive communication. One solution would have been to have that meeting once a week or even every other week and have a Daily Stand-up meeting for developers who were working on the same project. A Daily Stand-up meeting would have provided much more value to the developers and would have been shorter, and people would have paid more attention because the topics would directly relate to what they were working on.

Story 6: Inability to Share Knowledge

While on a small project with three Scrum teams, I saw first-hand how poor communication leads to a lot of wasted time. I was on one of the teams for only a few weeks when it became clear that all the teams had major communication issues. For example, one team had problems with the management of issues in its defect tracking system. One of the team leads held most of the information in his head, and the User Stories contained very few details. I was assigned one such User Story. When I wanted more details about the User Story I asked other team members. Everyone I asked said that only the team lead had knowledge about how a certain part of the application worked. This is an obvious case of "single point of failure," but even with that being the case the User Story could have contained comments that would have helped me work on it. Another situation that occurred often was being assigned a User Story for the current Sprint, where the User Story was marked as "not started." After working on one of these User Stories for several hours I was told that someone else was already looking into it. Again, time was wasted because something as simple as updating the status of the User Story hadn't been done. Poor communication comes in many forms, and since these teams relied so heavily (like most teams do) on an issue tracking system, it was one source of miscommunication.

Thoughts

Story 6 demonstrates how a few minutes of someone's time to add comments or update the status of a User Story could have saved hours and duplicated work and allowed the work to be started sooner. This may not sound like a big deal, but multiplied by several developers over months, it adds up.

The bottom line is that our tools are just one of the communication channels we use on teams, and that communication needs to be good. So take the time to make sure you are not a point of failure on your team: create documentation (the "teach others how to fish" metaphor), and make sure that you keep User Stories updated in whatever defect tracking tool you are using. It is a matter of discipline, but updating will improve communication on your team

Story 7: Simply Too Much Noise

On a large project there is always a chance for communication overload, which just creates noise. What I mean by "noise" is simply a lot of things that distract developers throughout the day and ultimately result in a lot of wasted time. I am not talking about the normal amount of company communication, e-mails, and chat rooms that we have all become accustomed to in software development; those just come with the territory.

On one large project, though, I saw an extreme misuse of communication channels and the amount of "noise" was ridiculous. For example, there were several e-mail distribution lists (developers only, architects, team leads, etc.). At first this worked, but over time people started sending things to the "everyone under the sun distribution" list. Literally hundreds of e-mails a day went out. Probably somewhere around 90% of these e-mails only pertained to 10–15% of the recipients. We also had many IRC channels and Skype rooms. But again, people started to use them in unintended ways that just created noise. People would tell jokes, and that would snowball into an hour-long comedy hour. That is great, but it is very frustrating when someone is trying to ask a legitimate question. It was not unusual to be away for ten minutes and come back to a Skype window and see hundreds of unread messages. In the end, most people just stopped watching the Skype rooms and IRC channels and filtered most e-mails.

Thoughts

There have been a lot of studies showing the cost of constantly being distracted throughout the workday and switching contexts. It all adds up to a lot of wasted time. I definitely experienced that, as I mentioned in Story 7. It was simply overwhelming. I think there are things that could have been done better. Following are some ideas of how things could have been done differently:

It would be better to educate people on using the right communication channel, not just what is easiest—the use of the right e-mail distribution lists, the use of the right IRC channels, and so on. Make this part of the onboard process for new hires on the project. Kindly remind people about using the correct communication channels when you spot misuse.

Something else that can help is to write succinct e-mails. There have been several articles written on this topic. One of my favorite suggestions is using just the subject line for short e-mails and putting "EOM" at the end of the subject line. EOM stands for "end of message." When people see EOM at the end of the subject line they know they don't need to open the e-mail and read it; they can just read the subject and then delete the e-mail. This probably saves three or four button clicks per e-mail. This is just one tip for using e-mail more efficiently, and there are a lot of great articles on this topic which are worth reading. One such article, by Brad Isaac, can be found at http://lifehacker.com/5028808/how-eom-makes-your-email-more-efficient.

When you are using Skype and are part of several groups, change the notification settings so that you only get an alert when certain words are entered into the conversation. Then, you can look at conversations that did not trigger a notification when you have time.

If a conversation in a Skype group or IRC channel really only pertains to a few individuals, take it offline into a new group or channel. This will help cut down on the amount of noise for all the others in the channel.

If you are fortunate to be co-located, have face-to-face meetings—which are much more valuable from my experience. Also, just get out of your seat and go talk to someone if he is close by. You get the added benefit of stretching your legs, too.

Story 8: A Common Language

Over the last 17 years or so I've worked with people from all over the world while at various companies. With these companies being located in the United States, knowing English was typically a requirement. At one of these companies, all the teams that worked on similar parts of the application sat in the same area. Co-location is one of the smartest things I think a company can do for Agile teams. It promotes conversations and you overhear things that you might not ever find out about had the team(s) not been co-located. It is a great way to increase productivity—at least that has been my experience. So, when I noticed that many conversations in this area where my team was located were taking place in Spanish, it made me wonder if this could have a negative effect. About a third of the team spoke English and Spanish and the rest of the team spoke English and perhaps one other language other than Spanish. When I heard these conversations, I wondered if what the developers were talking about would benefit the rest of the team. Would someone on the team be able to offer valuable information if he or she could understand the topic being discussed? Basically, I always wondered, "Is this harming the team in anyway?"

Thoughts

I think this is a sensitive area. No one wants to be the person to say, "Can you please use English." It might not come off as being a constructive suggestion. But I do think something is lost in a co-located team if people are not speaking a common language. For example, I was in Argentina for one company and I remember seeing the curious look on other developers' faces when some of us had work-related conversations in English. They wanted to be in on the conversation, as well they should be.

So, I think there is a polite way to simply ask team members to speak in a language that everyone can understand in that particular environment. It is nothing personal but is meant to help the team better communicate and get the most out of being co-located.

Story 9: Scrum Master Should Not Be a Part-Time Role

On many teams, a developer on the team or even the manager sometimes plays the role of Scrum Master. While I've seen this work in some instances, it can also hurt the Scrum team. For example, I was a member of a Scrum team where the manager played the Scrum Master role. The problem was that the manager had several teams and had a lot on her plate. Because of this, she would miss many of the Daily Stand-up meetings, at least for my team. This led to several instances where the manager was completely blindsided. I recall that during one Daily Stand-up meeting I mentioned that my User Story had some changes to its scope. I had mentioned this in several previous Daily Stand-up meetings, but the manager had not attended those meetings, so on this day when I mentioned it again, the manager was completely caught by surprise and not too happy.

Thoughts

The point of the Daily Stand-up meeting is to share information, understand what each member of the team is doing, and work together to remove any barriers. It is a time for the team to decide what is the best way to tackle the day's work. It is also for the Scrum Master to make sure the team is not blocked, to make sure everyone on the team is getting what he needs. It is critical that whoever is playing the Scrum Master role attend all the Daily Stand-up meetings. In Story 9there were really two issues. The first issue was that the manager could not dedicate enough time required to the role of Scrum Master. The second issue was that the manager was not aware of what the team was doing and therefore did not know whether the team was having blocking issues.

Fortunately, the Scrum team I was on was pretty seasoned, so the surprises to the manager were not frequent. But I can imagine a situation where this type of disconnect could be a much larger issue for less seasoned teams. The bottom line is that the Scrum Master role is a full-time role and is critical to the success of Agile teams.

Poor Foundations

What can be done early on to set your teams up for success? What kinds of things are worth investing time in and how much do you try to solve for not knowing exactly what is needed in the long run? Furthermore, how do you front load a project with all the foundational-type work (think continuous integration, frameworks, etc.) that will make the rest of the project go smoothly? Once you think you know what those things are, how do you convince management that this upfront cost will pay off in the long run? One thing is fairly certain: if you don't invest in a solid foundation your Agile project will pay for it in the long run.

Real-Life Stories

Story 1: Building a Good Foundation

I was fortunate to be a technical lead of a team that was one of the first to start work on a multiyear, multi-million-dollar project. This team had an initial set of foundational items to complete that would pave the way for the rest of the development teams once they joined. Some of the things we started work on were caching frameworks, analytics frameworks, setting up Continuous Integration (CI) plans, and picking code-quality tools like Clover and PMD. There were some other teams working on similar items. Unfortunately, a decision was made to kick off the development for this project without completing many of the foundational items. Keep in mind that on a large project like this, once development starts it is very hard to stop development and work on foundational-type items. Furthermore, once teams started using frameworks that were incomplete, it was very hard to go back and switch to newer versions of those frameworks. As you can imagine, this created a lot of technical debt. In my experience, "this will get fixed later" usually means it will never get fixed.

Thoughts

In the beginning of a project there is a lot to think about. I think the items discussed next are worth at least thinking about. Of course, you're going to get some things wrong. But doing some of these things can minimize the pain.

Put some serious thought into CI, if not Continuous Delivery (CD). There are many excellent resources on this topic, including *Continuous Delivery* by Jez Humble and David Farley (Pearson Education, 2011). This book explains the reasons for CI, some different approaches to automated testing, the various stages in a typical CI pipeline, and so on. Not all groups will need a full CI pipeline, but having even a basic CI pipeline setup for a codebase that has several developers (and you are trying to create software that is potentially shippable at the end of the Sprint) is vital.

As part of your CI strategy, it is important to set up the code quality gates for the project. This does a few things: makes sure all developers are following the same standards, helps prevent bugs, reduces technical debt, and ensures code is being adequately tested.

Put some thought into the processes your team uses. I do not believe this is in direct opposition to the Agile principle of "value people over process." I am not talking about building in tons of process or anything that would build barriers to communication. Of course, you're not going to get everything right; that is the purpose of Retrospectives and the chance to change things during every Sprint. But some things to think about are code review processes, architecture guidelines, and workflows (like those in Jira®) for moving a User Story through the normal User Story states. Another thing to think about is documenting the "Steps to Doneness," which can help to make sure everyone is on the same page in terms of what "Done Done" means. Finally, it is good to have some process or agreement around writing automated functional testing.

Leaning on the knowledge of people who have experience using Agile can be very helpful—maybe an Agile Coach or someone on the team who takes the time to do the research and bring that knowledge back to the team. Learning from the mistakes of other teams/experts will go a long way to putting the team on the right track.

These processes are critical to have in place and not putting thought into them upfront will typically cost the project in the long run. Some people would say this concept is anti-Agile, but I don't think that is the case. There is nothing in the Agile principles that say we don't need to do design or set up foundational items. In fact, I think not doing so is one of the biggest mistakes that new Agile teams make.

So what are some of the ways we can tackle these items?

Set aside a "Sprint 0" to tackle foundational-type items or to set up your processes. This Sprint is usually a "free" Sprint where the team's velocity will not be measured and the User Stories don't necessarily have direct business value.

Scrum embraces a concept of Spikes, and Spikes can be used to tackle research-type items or some of these types of foundational items. Spikes are similar to the "risk mitigation" in the Elaboration phase we used to use in RUP. Spikes should be used sparingly and are the exception, not the rule.

Dedicate teams to building out foundational items at the beginning of the project. On smaller projects, having a Sprint 0 might be sufficient. On larger projects, it might take a few Sprints.

In some companies you might have an architecture or advanced technologies group that can be engaged to help with some of these types of items. Use Sprint 0 or Spikes to talk with these teams and find out what they have that can be leveraged based on your platform needs.

Story 2: Rigid Rules

Sometimes even the best of intentions can lead to very bad results. I saw an example of this on an Agile project where the architecture team put in place the quality gates for the client, which was on a LAMP stack. One of the mandates was that all PHP code had to have code coverage. That sounds great on the surface. But there were a few issues: (1) the web developers were not used to writing unit tests and (2) the code coverage number was a blanket number and did not take into account complexity, maintainability, or if the tests actually achieved anything. This led to tests that were hard to maintain and added very little value. Even worse, it led to perfectly good code being refactored just to allow for unit testing. Even with these side effects and the grumblings of the web developers, management did not want to change the code coverage floor.

It was not until toward the end of the project that team finally moved to using the CRAP (Change Risk Analysis and Prediction) metric in PHPUnit, which focused on testing complex code. By that point many brittle unit tests had been written and eventually deleted.

There had been so much wasted time and effort just because one group mandated 100% code coverage and then never followed up to see how this process was working in practice.

Thoughts

Putting quality standards in place is important, and in this case the intentions were good. Following are a few things that could have saved this project a lot of time and money:

One of the lessons learned from this project was to make a good case to management early on when you see red flags. Build a coalition of other developers who see the same issues. Form a proposal and show why things should be changed. If you can show that money will be saved and developers will be more productive, management should be willing to listen.

One way to address the lack of confidence in the application would have been to have adequate automated functional tests. Unfortunately, in this case, the automated functional tests were also lacking. I think that if an Agile team is doing behavior-driven development (BDD), there is an argument that you don't need as many unit tests. If the automated functional tests are good, then you can have confidence that the application is behaving as expected. That is a better measure than pure code coverage (90% code coverage of an application that does not behave as expected does not mean much to the user).

Long-Run Plan for Success

So what happens when the project goes live and people start rolling off? Is all that knowledge lost? How do you stop the "I didn't write this crap" mentality from setting in. I can't even count how many times I've heard that phrase. I've heard so many developers use the "I wasn't involved in that decision, so I'm just going to follow what they did" excuse instead of refactoring a bad piece of code. This doesn't fall into a single clean Agile category, but it affects things like code quality, morale, and ultimately the productivity of teams, so I thought it would be good idea to cover it in this book.

Real-Life Stories

Story 1: Creating a Sense of Ownership

On a very large project I saw the effect of what I just described in the introduction to this chapter. We used several vendors and contractors to pump out code. One of the vendors, which will go un-named, had a small army of analysts and developers on the project. To be clear, these were very talented individuals for the most part. . But at the end of the day, these individuals were under a lot of pressure to get code delivered and knew full well that they would not be supporting this application when it went live. Sure enough, there was a lot of poorly written and designed code. To compound the issue, there was no real documentation and these developers were the only ones who knew how key parts of the application worked. Once the project went live and the vendor, and other individual contractors, rolled off the project, it was apparent that what the vendor and the contractors delivered had a lot of issues. Of course, it was too late at that point and the employees of the company were stuck having to learn this code and then replace large portions of it.

Thoughts

Again, this problem is not all that unique. What makes it interesting is that it is not unexpected, yet proper planning to account for it is often not put in place. But there are things that can be done to minimize such problems.

For example, think about some sort of oversight. Have senior developers from the company provide oversight for architecture and design decisions. Have code reviews that must be signed off on by at least one senior developer.

Another thing to think about is accountability. Have something in the contract language about holding vendors accountable for what they deliver. There should be something in the contract about accepted code coverage numbers, defect counts, and so on.

Give some thought to effective handoff requirements. The contract language should include something about handoff requirements, and about creating handoff documentation in the companies' required format. Such documentation should be reviewed with the teams that will support the code after it goes live.

Finally, put coding standards in place. Having standards in place, as I've talked about elsewhere in this book, is crucial. These standards should be enforced in code reviews and through CI (via static analysis and automated tests).

Story 2: Spreading Knowledge

In another organization I saw the impact of offshoring sustainment. We had several teams in South America that supported part of the application. These teams were very good and knew parts of the application very well. The problem was that whenever there was a holiday in their country (apparently the country has a lot of them), there was no coverage if there was a live site (production outage). Specifically, there was no primary off-hours developer. When a production issue arose during one of these holidays, a manager had to scramble to find a developer who could look into the issue. This was not good for the business because the response time was slow, not good for the manager who had to run around to find someone to help, and finally not good for the poor developer who had a trial by fire.

Thoughts

I don't think the situation in Story 2 is all that unique to this one organization or company. I've seen application support offshored at other companies. But I think a few things can be done to mitigate this risk to the business.

For example, either have the offshore team take care of 24/7 support or have an onshore team lead. 24/7 support obviously addresses the issue, but I would still recommend doing some of the other things mentioned, like cross-pollination. The onshore team lead is something I think is a good idea in general, not just in terms of support.

Another idea is to have documentation (troubleshooting guides, procedures, etc.) that can be used by other teams to support parts of the application when the primary teams are not available.

Try rotating the support among offshore and onshore teams. That way when one of the offshore teams is not available, there would be an onshore team that at least has the knowledge needed to support a production issue. This type of "cross-pollination" among teams is a good thing in general.

Story 3: Good Transition of Ownership

In contrast to Story 1, about what happens when contractors and vendors roll off a project and there is no transition, I was on a project where I saw the opposite happen. On that project, granted it was a smaller project of about 30 developers, the transition to the sustainment team was baked into the project plan from the beginning. The other thing that was different was that the project team and sustainment team were two different groups with different managers.

The manager of the sustainment team essentially would not agree to take on supporting the new application until a proper handoff was done. By the time the new application went live, a very smooth transition was done to the sustainment team.

This project was an Agile project, specifically Kanban, but regardless of being Agile or not, a smooth transition is important to the long-run success of whatever team is going to support the application.

Thoughts

So what are some of the factors that led to this smooth transition?

- We put together handoff documentation

- We had meetings with the teams that were taking over the application. In these meetings we went over the documentation we created and we discussed the application and infrastructure architecture and how to troubleshoot the application.

- This project had invested heavily in BDD, and when we handed off the application we had the functional tests running and green. Having automated functional tests is great whether you are handing off an application or the same team that built the application is supporting it. But in the case of handing off the support, if the automated functional tests are green in your CI pipeline, like unit tests, it tells the team members that they have not broken expected behavior, and the new sustainment team will have a sense of confidence.

- We had a clean product backlog with items prioritized. This made the transition of support after launch very smooth. Transitions of applications are often not just the application at a code level but can be at a Product Owner level, so having a clean Product Backlog matters.

CHAPTER

6

Adjusting in Time

The value of adaptability is one of the core concepts in Agile. Adaptability embraces the idea of not being so rigid in terms of delivering functionality that you can't change midstream. It's also being able to recognize when things are heading in the wrong direction and adjusting before it is too late. It is about staying flexible, but doing it in a way that does not waste the team's time.

Real-Life Stories

Story 1: Planning Too Far Ahead

After a few weeks of being on a new Scrum team I noticed that the team had an interesting way of planning work. Basically, on the Monday before the Sprint ended all the team members would disappear for a few hours. I asked my technical lead if I was missing an invite on my calendar. He told me that I was, and then I asked, "OK. What meeting is this on every other Monday?" He explained to me that it was the "Sprint Readiness" meeting. Being a Certified Scrum Master (CSM) and having been on several Agile teams, I was curious about the purpose of this meeting. In the next Sprint Readiness meeting the team met in a room and our SDET (Software Developer in Test) started to go through some of the User Stories from the Product Backlog. When I asked if these were for the next Sprint, he explained that they were for two Sprints in the future. I found this a bit odd, having seen in the past that is hard to predict what the business would need during the next Sprint, never mind during two Sprints in the future. But this was a process that the team had established, and so the team members held the meeting like clockwork. It didn't matter if all the User Stories we reviewed never even made it into the anticipated Sprint.

It's possible, and in fact it did happen, that User Stories we reviewed never made it into any Sprint. I tried to point out some of the shortcomings of this meeting and possible alternative approaches, but this particular team seemed pretty set in its ways.

Thoughts

The team wasted a lot of time in these meetings and even when the User Stories did make it into the intended Sprint they were not ready. I think the following are some things that could have been tried and would have resulted in a better use of time and added more value:

In general, a Scrum team should not try to predict what the business will want beyond two weeks in the future. Things simply change too often to try to predict beyond the two weeks. That is why the Product Owner should be prioritizing the Product Backlog and then in Sprint Planning should tell the team what he or she wants to be worked on in the next Sprint.

One approach I've used that worked well was to have a "pre-Sprint Planning" meeting. This was held a few days before the Sprint Planning meeting. Typically only the leads (tech lead, BA lead, and QA lead) would attend this meeting, but that was just because of how the team was structured. The idea of the meeting was to look at the stories the Product Owner thought he wanted in the next Sprint. Since it was a few days before the Sprint Planning meeting, this tended to be pretty accurate. We would go through these User Stories and make sure they had everything they needed to be brought into the next Sprint (acceptance criteria, comps, and annotations, etc.). This made the Sprint Planning meeting go a lot quicker.

Regardless of whether you just have a regular Sprint Planning or some sort of a "pre-Sprint planning" meeting, I think it is best run by the Product Owner (or BA proxy). It provides an opportunity for the team to ask questions and make sure team members understand exactly the scope of each User Story.

Story 2: Always Be Improving

One of the things I like about Agile is the idea of constant improvement. Specifically, I like the Retrospective meeting. But I've been on teams where this meeting was slowly being phased out. For example, I was on one Scrum team whose members eventually started skipping the Retrospective meeting altogether. Team members felt that the meeting was just not adding any value and the developers would rather be back at their desks. It started with just skipping the Retrospective once or twice, but then it became usual to not have the meeting. Not only should this team not have proclaimed to be a Scrum team, but I think its members were really missing out on an opportunity to improve the team.

Thoughts

In this example, I think it was as much a matter of the team not understanding the value of having the Retrospective as it was laziness on the part of some of the team members.

Whether you are following Scrum or some other flavor of Agile, the concept of stopping at the end of each iteration and seeing what went well and what didn't is important. If this isn't happening, the team is missing an opportunity for improvement.

This meeting can be ongoing and doesn't have to be formal, but I do find that having a meeting time set aside helps to get the team together even when there are a lot of other things going on.

There are many ways to run Retrospective meetings and many ways to decide on the biggest pain points. Typically I've seen teams vote on the top three negative items. One thing I don't always see is follow-up on these negative items. So I've created "follow-up items" and I assign them to team members. They are tracked on the task board (either physical or virtual). This keeps the items visible and there is a better chance that they are not forgotten. If they are acted on, then whatever pain points were experienced should go away in the next Sprint. Over time, the velocity of the team will increase as a result of removing these pain points.

Story 3: A Lot of Wasted Planning

While on a Scrum team that was starting a new e-commerce project, I noticed that the team members did something that seemed contrary to what I've seen work on other Agile projects. This particular team had estimated the User Stories in the Product Backlog and was getting ready for the first Sprint Planning meeting. The project manager scheduled a "multi-Sprint Planning meeting" for the week before the typical Sprint Planning meeting. I thought to myself, "I wonder what this meeting is going to be all about?" As it turns out, the meeting was just as the invite said; it was to take the User Stories from the Product Backlog and try to plan out all the Sprints for the project. I've seen teams do dependency mapping exercises, which makes sense so that you understand the order in which the stories need to be worked. But trying to plan multiple Sprints on a whiteboard did not seem to make much sense. What are the chances that the priority of the User Stories won't change or that some of the stories won't get descoped? Well, as it turns out the chances were pretty good.

Thoughts

I've worked on some Agile projects where we would map out all remaining Sprints and try to map out what would go in each Sprint. But this would typically happen later in the project and only when the backlog was pretty well groomed and more or less stable. In those cases, it was more to see if all the stories could fit into the remaining Sprints, not to come up with a "plan" for all Sprints. Even then, what was mapped out did not end up matching what actually happened.

I think, in general, a Scrum team should not try to predict what the business will want beyond two weeks in the future. Things simply change too often to try to plan the work for the next two Sprints, never mind the next ten Sprints. Even with two-week Sprints things can change, and the Product Owner comes yelling, "But I need to get this other User Story done during this Sprint." Most teams manage this by having a rule that the Product Owner can swap things of equal point value and only if the User Story being swapped out is not yet started. This is more a Kanban style, but I think it can be used in Scrum if it is the exception now and then.

I think it is better to make sure the Product Backlog is groomed well. This way you do not waste time going through User Stories that are no longer needed, are lower priority, and so on. If the Product Owner is going through and making sure the Product Backlog is being prioritized and if the team is having the Sprint Planning meeting, then I think that is sufficient. If you want to map out all the Sprints and follow a more or less rigid plan, that is fine, but then don't call it Agile. Maybe it is more of a Water-Scrum-fall model (as described by Dave West of Forrester Research), which might work better in your organization. Water-Scrum-fall is a term I've started seeing more and more as companies have adopted Agile. Basically, it means that a project is being run like a traditional Waterfall project but is also using parts of Scrum. For example, there might be two-week Sprints and the typical Scrum meetings might be conducted, but the delivery of the software follows more of a Waterfall model where it is tested and deployed to Production at the end of the project.

Sending the Wrong Signals

How does an organization that is adopting Agile show that it is serious about adopting Agile values and principles? How does management avoid sending the wrong signals to teams—signals that are confusing and contradict what people have learned about Agile on their own or at other companies? Sending the wrong signals can lead to a lot of confusion and can create poor morale among teams. Poor morale can then lead to poor-quality software and spending more time on things like technical debt. This is the opposite of building projects around motivated individuals and giving them what they need to be successful.

Real-Life Stories

Story 1: Complete Breakdown in Trust

While working on a large project that had adopted BDD, I personally experienced how sending the wrong signals can lead to a complete breakdown in trust.

On this project we had requirements that said that every feature needed automated functional tests. This sounded great in theory, but unfortunately team members lacked the discipline to maintain the automated tests. At one point, when tests started to fail often and it became clear that we needed dedicated developers to maintain the tests, management chose to stop running the automated tests. This led to many automated tests becoming outdated very quickly. It also led to an increase in introduced defects, which in turn led to low confidence in the software we were delivering. This ultimately led to more and more manual testing. It also engendered a feeling among teams that they had wasted so much time on tests that were now rotting on the vine. The other feeling that started to spread among Agile teams was a lack of trust in management's dedication to delivering quality software.

Thoughts

In Story 1, this was a real turning point in terms of team morale. There was already some mistrust of management and how the project was being run, but the decision to lower our standards really created a bad atmosphere that would last until the end of the project.

A different approach may have been to take the following into consideration: first, set realistic goals upfront and base them on past experience. Don't base these goals on some other company's standards. Setting the bar high is one thing, but given your team's skill sets and past performance, be realistic in your quality gates.

Second, perhaps start small and build on success. In other words, set realistic quality gates and then ramp up a little over time to raise the bar. For example, make it a rule that code coverage can never go down once it hits a new level. So, if the project says you need to have 80% code coverage, set that as your floor. As you add more tests and the coverage goes up to, let's say, 85%, set that as the new floor and don't allow developers to lower the floor.

Finally, as mentioned in Chapter 4, building a solid foundation is critical to the success of your Agile teams. Don't set your teams up for failure. Telling teams that they need to write automated functional tests without having the appropriate infrastructure and support will only lead to failure for the teams. Instead, invest in the needed infrastructure and support so that they scale as more tests are added.

Instead of completely stopping the automated testing, management could have formed a team whose sole focus was to create and maintain the automated tests.

This is just one idea. The point is to find solutions that do not undermine your Agile team's ability to deliver quality software.

I'm a big believer in automated tests (unit, functional, and integration) and think that for any company or organization to be successful, it needs to be willing to invest in testing. The ROI (return on investment) can be huge: catching defects early in CI, less manual testing, speed to market, and so on.

Story 2: Please Don't Compare Scrum Teams

While training to become a CSM, I had learned that Scrum teams should not be compared. Each team has its own velocity, its own way of estimating User Stories, and its own idea of what a point represents. But I saw the exact opposite on one Agile project.

On this specific project managers thought that one way to get the teams to perform better would be to compare teams' velocities. By all accounts, that is a truly terrible idea, regardless of what is taught in Scrum Master certification. The comparing of velocities led to a lot of terrible things on this specific project. It led to teams inflating their point values just to say they closed more points than other teams. I recall looking at a User Story from one team that was 8 points and thought to myself, "This would be equivalent to a 3-point story on my team." It led to teams cramming through code that was not ready. It led to bitter feelings between teams; I heard things like "the X team thinks they are so much better, but they really suck."

I remember saying to my manager at one point, "Comparing points across teams means nothing. It doesn't tell the whole story. A team's health and velocity should be the real measure of success." He was not very happy with that comment. Soon other developers started saying "points don't matter." There was no convincing some managers and the team comparisons continued. But by the end of the project most developers could care less about being compared to other teams and knew it meant nothing.

Thoughts

At the end of the day there was a huge misunderstanding, I believe, on the part of management when it came to thinking that comparing teams would create some kind of healthy competition. It had so many unforeseen consequences. Having a slide that shows how many points each team closed each Sprint created less team unity, not more. The teams on that particular project were in many geographic areas, so it also led to an "us vs. them" mentality.

Having a presentation slide showing the Sprint point commitment and what the team actually closed is fine. But instead of comparing team's velocities, show the velocity of each team over the last three Sprints. Show how they are doing as a team, not compared to some other team.

The reason comparing teams did not work on this project, and I suspect would not work in most organizations, is that each team estimated the User Stories in their backlog (which is the way it should be) and a 3-point story for one team might be a 5-point story for another.

I suppose if you are in an organization that wants to compare Agile teams, just don't get caught up in it, and understand that it is the health of your team that is truly important.

Story 3: Dictating Velocity

One of the things we learn about in Agile is how velocity plays a major role. We use velocity to plan Sprint commitments, to balance life and work, and to gauge how well the team is improving over time. While on a project, I saw the exact opposite—instead of velocity being used to gauge what a team could commit to in a Sprint, program management began to dictate how many points each team must close.

The teams had to meet these commitments, even if it meant working late nights and weekends. It didn't matter what the velocity of the teams had been up to that point; each team needed to complete X points per Sprint. Teams were treated as failures if they did not meet these mandated Sprint commitments.

This process caused so much distrust and lack of respect for leadership. It really created a terrible work environment that would last until the end of the project.

Thoughts

One thing we know is that working late hours leads to mistakes. No matter how good you are, when you are tired, you will make mistakes. As developers we are not immune to this (we might like to think we are superhuman, but alas we are not). I remember many times working late into the night. The next day or week I'd look at the code and think, "What was I thinking?" The mentality of mandating a Sprint commitment and having people work insane hours led to what I had seen in my own code, but it was multiplied by hundreds of developers.

As you might guess, the quality of the code went downhill fast. It was functionally correct in the sense that it did what it was supposed to, most of the time. But things like code coverage, well-designed code, and so on, suffered. Ultimately, these things made the application hard to maintain. Not surprisingly, after about a year in Production there was talk of doing major rewrites of portions of the application.

As you might imagine, the morale of the developers was not that great after the practice of mandating Sprint commitments began. It is only empirical, but I would say productivity did go down.

Every project has deadlines, and that is not going away. But if you tell teams that you are adopting Scrum and that they can have a better work-life balance by using velocity as a measure, then live up to that promise. Knowing the velocity of each team should in fact allow program managers to know exactly how the project is tracking. Just as we use burn-down charts for an Agile team to show the Product Owner how things are going, we can use project level burn-downs to see how the project is tracking and then it is transparent to executives. With this information there is no reason to not adjust sooner and avoid the "death marches" that many of us are so used to seeing.

Story 4: Avoid Creating Team Hierarchies

While in one organization, I saw some teams say that they were Scrum teams with a flat structure, but in reality that was not the case. The team I was on had a "technical/team lead" role and even though everyone on the team was supposed to be equal, this one person made most of the decisions. Generally speaking, this person's opinion mattered more than that of other team members. In fact, instead of team members being more self-organized and self-sufficient, they depended heavily on this one person for handing out work.

Thoughts

In Scrum, no person on the team is supposed to have more power than the others. I like the idea of having everyone as equals on the team. Even the Scrum Master does not have more power than others on the Scrum team. But what I saw on this team, and others within this organization, was that the majority of decisions fell to the team lead.

One concept I read about when I was first learning Agile was self-organizing teams: the idea that the team can determine the best way to get things done. But even when a team is highly self-organized, there is still a need for a manager. One of the things a manager can do is to make sure an Agile team is functioning and that is the team has a balance of power. For example, if there is a really strong personality on the team who is convincing everyone to go in her direction all the time, that is not good. In this instance, a manager can perhaps introduce another strong personality on the team to equal things out. Or, the manager can put processes into place that can help to make sure everyone on the team is being heard. Planning Poker when estimating can be one such method.

The main point is to make sure everyone on the team feels he has an equal voice in the decisions that affect the team. When using Planning Poker, for example, if there is a disagreement on how many story points should be assigned to a User Story, each team member can give his reasons for the estimation and the team can come to a consensus.

Balancing Life and Work

One of the promises of Agile is a better work-life balance. But even with Agile this is not always the case. Sometimes projects are called "Agile projects" but are run just like a RUP or Waterfall-managed project. There can be "death marches" at the end of the project and work-life balance goes out the window. Other times there can be extreme peaks and valleys. These are not unique to using Agile by any means, but the question is, How can we use the Agile methodology more effectively to truly have a better work-life balance?

Real-Life Stories

Story 1: Mandating Velocity

I was on a newly formed Scrum team and saw first-hand how the use of velocity really led to a better work-life balance. This Scrum team, like other new Scrum teams I had been on, started off kind of rough. We did not initially meet our Sprint commitments and had trouble estimating User Stories. Over time our velocity improved and eventually became pretty predictable. But then something unfortunate happened: program management decided that the project deadlines were not going to be met, so they started to mandate Sprint commitments for teams. They knew for some teams this might mean closing 25% or even 50% more points in a Sprint. So, in order to accomplish this there was also mandatory overtime. At first we were told we just had to work four weekends in a row. Then it became six weekends. Then it became open-ended. Developers were working 13 hours a day plus weekends. All the talk of work-life balance completely went out the window.

Having enjoyed the early success on our Scrum team of using the team's velocity to not overload the team, adjusting to this new way of working was painful. It is not that as developers we don't have to work some long hours—that is fine (from time to time). But when it becomes the norm, it burns people out and can really kill team morale.

Thoughts

One of the ways we can achieve a better work-life balance using Agile is through the use of velocity. Velocity is a tool for capacity planning and ideally can be used to make sure the team does not overcommit to work. It's not unusual for developers to overcommit (yes, we like to please managers and will sometimes say we can do in one day what takes three). The use of relative sizing (discussed in more detail in Chapter 13) along with a team's velocity can help ensure that a team does not take on more work than it has historically been able to complete in a Sprint. If used correctly, and the team is the one making the Sprint commitment, then this can lead to a better work-life balance.

Of course, like anything else, the idea of using velocity as a planning tool can be gamed. So it is important that managers keep the team honest. The team will probably have a lower velocity when it is first formed, but every Sprint the velocity should get better—until it hits a plateau. Once that happens it will become harder to increase velocity, but it can be achieved by squeezing out waste from your processes. Of course, the velocity can take a hit for various reasons (unforeseen impediments, when team members leave, onboarding new team members, etc.). Also, make sure to do capacity planning during your Sprint Planning. This is not a technique that all Scrum Masters follow, but I've seen it work well. It means that before you make your Sprint commitment, take into account things like planned vacations, appointments, meetings, and so on. For example, if several people have vacation days during a Sprint, of course your Sprint commitment will be lower than your historical velocity, and that should be expected. As long as the Sprint commitment is lower for legitimate reasons, the team should not feel bad.

The bottom line is that if used properly, the tools we have with Agile can lead to a much better work-life balance for everyone on an Agile team.

Story 2: Creating a Cadence

Extreme peaks and valleys also disrupt work-life balance. I've seen this, to one degree or another, since I first started as a developer. I saw it earlier on when using Waterfall and then RUP. But when I started using Agile I saw fewer of these peaks and valleys. However, on one Scrum team I saw really bad peaks and valleys. A lot of these peaks and valleys came as a result of the way this

organization did its funding. On this Scrum team we would work on a project for a while. When the project ended we would then have no work. The
manager would tell us to find "filler work." We would go weeks, or in one
case over a month, without pulling things from the Product Backlog. Because
of this, we had velocity per se. We randomly worked on things in the Sprint.
Then a new project would get approved and all of sudden we were given a lot
of work with a tight deadline. So we would go from not having any work to
now working long hours.

There was no cadence on this team. We had no historical velocity we could
trust. Even if the team wanted to commit to points based on historical velocity we couldn't because there simply were not enough stories in the Product
Backlog.

Thoughts

There was obviously a much bigger issue in the story. But in this particular
organization, I talked to developers on other teams who were experiencing
the same issues. However, even with the unique funding model of this organization, I think things could have been done differently to provide a better
work-life balance.

One issue is whether Agile teams are 100% dedicated to projects or dedicated 100% to sustainment. If a team is 100% funded by project work, then
it is likely there will be these kinds of peaks and valleys. Having a team split
between project and sustainment work can be one solution. For example, we
have a Product Backlog, and use Epics to divide project work and sustainment
work (i.e., defect fixes and improvements). Then the team pulls from these
two Epics (or maybe uses components or whatever makes sense in its environment) and commits to points based on its historical velocity. This does
not have to be a 50/50 mixture. Maybe at times it is 80% project work and
20% sustainment and then 100% sustainment when there is no project work.
This is just one possible solution, but the point is to find a way to have a good
work-life balance and for the team to have a steady cadence.

Story 3: Great Work-Life Balance

While on a Scrum team that had been together for about eight months, I saw
one of the best examples of work-life balance on an Agile project that I had
ever seen. We were a cross-functional team (development, QA, business analysis) and we had several processes in place after eight months. Then we were
told the project would be shelved and that we were moving onto a new high-
priority project that had extremely tight deadlines. We switched from Scrum
to Kanban (using Scrum meetings and a Work-In-Progress (WIP) limit and we
had Service Level Agreements (SLA) based on point values). During Sprint

Planning the team was really given full control of the Sprint commitment. We looked at our velocity from the last Sprint and our historical velocities and then planned out our Sprint. We were encouraged to keep improving and to commit to more points than the previous Sprint, but were not forced to do it.

The other thing that was key in terms of a work-life balance was the support of management. Both the technical manager and the project manager were very insistent that people go home at a decent time every day. This was because this particular organization had a history of projects with "death marches." Leadership knew that death marches killed morale and they were determined that this Agile project would be run differently.

Thoughts

The project described in Story 3 became the gold standard for an Agile project within this particular organization. In large part this was due to the lack of stress and great work-life balance that everyone on the team felt. Even with launching on time and on budget, we had, maybe, two weekends of extra hours over seven months. We launched with very few high-priority defects (definitely no functional defects).

The key was letting the team decide what to commit to each Sprint. The team knew the amount of work for the project was not changing (i.e., everything that could be descoped was already removed), but team members were allowed to decide how much they could take on each Sprint. This led to transparency with the business, which meant no surprises. It was then up to management to decide how to handle any gaps between projected velocity and the deadline.

The other key to this Agile's project success was management's support. Hearing from a technical manager that it's OK to leave at 5 p.m. and to not burn yourself out was refreshing. On so many software delivery projects (Agile or otherwise) it is all about getting something out the door, no matter the human cost (I talk about such a project and the detrimental effects it had on developers in Chapter 7). In a strange way, lack of pressure actually made everyone on the project work harder and do better work.

Fake It Until You Make It

Because Agile has become the new "hot" trend over the last few years, it is tempting for an organization to just jump to saying "yes, we are doing Agile." I've seen in several organizations where they rename a meeting a "morning Scrum," and suddenly the organization is "doing Agile." Sometimes it is just a misunderstanding of what Agile is all about. Other times it is more blatant. There are many things that are important for an organization to do as it adopts the Agile development methodology. Things like education and experience are important to the successful transition to Agile software development. Using buzzwords is not enough.

Real-Life Stories

Story 1: Not Shippable

I've been on several Scrum teams that, in reality, were using Water-Scrum-fall. What I mean is that on these teams, we were having the Scrum meetings, we were doing estimations, we were using BDD, and so on. However, when the demo meeting came around, we would show the Product Owner what was built and collect the points for those User Stories, but the reality is that what we had built was nowhere near shippable. We had "Steps to Doneness" that talked about quality standards, testing, and signoff by the Product Owner. But all these things overlooked a huge aspect: vertical integration. It was the elephant in the room on these teams and projects. Everyone knew that what was being demo-ed was not shippable, or even potentially shippable. This is because integration across multiple systems/services was not completed yet. Once we started integrating all the various layers in the application and across system boundaries, we easily had months of work left before the application could be shipped. This is why I would call it Water-Scrum-fall and not Scrum. I would argue that this should not be called Agile either, but management loved to call these successful Agile projects.

Thoughts

At the end of the Sprint, I think a Scrum team should have a shippable product. If not, then I don't think your business is getting the most out of Agile. Delivering business value in an incremental way is one of the things I like most about Agile. The idea that development teams can deliver business value in small, incremental ways is one of the major benefits of using Agile.

Just completing a Sprint and meeting your point commitment is not really the point (no pun intended). Teams need to be honest about what is being demo-ed. If integration is not complete and some things are mocked, then team members clearly need to explain that to the organization. They must explain that even though the story was completed, it is not shippable and it will be shippable when story X is completed. As long as the business partners and the development teams are on the same page, there is no misrepresentation of what is being delivered.

There are plenty of articles on the value of CI and the role it plays in Agile, so I won't go into detail here. But in a nutshell, the idea is that when you have a green build, what you are saying is that the product you just built is "potentially" shippable. The idea is to do integration early and often because doing the integration later is more painful. In most environments I've been in, the artifact built in the CI pipeline says we have something that "could" be deployed to Production. However, it usually does not go directly to Production without some sort of manual intervention. I'm only talking about CI here, and not CD. But in Story 1, a green CI build really meant nothing. Between inadequate functional testing and the fact that new features were not always fully integrated, the artifact built in the CI pipeline gave no real confidence that we could deploy it to Production.

So, the bottom line is to call a spade a spade. If you are practicing Water-Scrum-fall, that is fine, but don't claim that you are practicing Scrum. Don't claim to be delivering business value every two weeks when you are not building shippable software.

Story 2: Functional Software

While on one e-commerce project, there was a mandate that everyone check into the mainline branch. This is because checking in code early and often into a mainline (or what some call trunk-based development) is generally a good practice. The thinking is that by using one branch for all development it forces developers to integrate their code. This will raise issues/defects early on instead of postponing the integration until later. On this particular project the way we prevented new features from showing in Production was to use Feature Toggles. There is plenty of information on using Feature Toggles, but the gist of it is that you "hide" new features behind a toggle (it can be anything from an "if" statement or using some declarative mechanism like an XML file). You have the Feature Toggles "off" until you are ready to expose the new functionality and then toggle the feature "on."

One of the main reasons this approach was chosen was that "this is how the big tech companies do it." So if we do what they are doing, we must be Agile, right? Well, no.

Having used this approach on several projects where the mainline was a live application and we had several parallel projects going on, I can say it does not work. We had hundreds of toggles in the user interface and these toggles were never cleaned up. The other issue was that changes for projects were constantly breaking the application in Production. This was an e-commerce application, so these defects sometimes impacted revenue. We also had RESTful services, each in its own mainline branch. The problem was there was no toggle mechanism in these services. So code related to projects that might not go live for months was actually "live" code in Production.

Thoughts

In Story 2, the mainline development and use of toggles was somewhat of a knee-jerk reaction by the architecture team to the use of Feature Branches. I tend to agree with Martin Fowler's comment, "Release toggles are a useful technique and a lot of teams use them. However they should be your last choice when you're dealing with putting features into production." On these specific Agile project teams we were using Feature Branches for every User Story. Our SCM (source configuration management) was Perforce, so each Feature Branch was what is called a "hard" branch. As you can imagine, for a set of features taking months to complete, the amount of Feature Branches in Perforce grew significantly and the merging of these branches back into the main branch was painful.

Instead of using Feature Toggles or Feature Branches when you have parallel projects and sustainment all checking into the same branch, I recommend using Project Branches. You can think of these as Feature Branches, but at higher level. So instead of having a branch per long-running feature, you have a branch for long-running projects. Then, within each Project Branch you treat it as a mainline (check in early and often, run through CI on each commit, etc.).

But projects can run many months, and the whole time the main branch is having check-ins by the sustainment team. And other Project Branches are also moving along with changes. So how do you avoid merging at the end of the project when the pain of merging can be complete hell due to the amount of changes in each branch? One possible answer is to do merges down from the main branch into your Project Branch. Do this as part of the development iteration (i.e., the Sprint) so that the project branch never falls too far behind the main branch and merges should be less painful. This is a kind of hybrid approach of mainline development and Feature Branches, but it removes the need for toggles. That is not to say that toggles aren't great and can be used for other purposes, but with the foregoing approach we don't need hundreds of them littering the code base.

There is no single branching and merging strategy that will work for all teams. There are so many variables: SCM tool being used, team structure, how releases are scheduled, and so on. But the point is that checking code into a main branch and pushing it to Production when it is not meant to go live for months is a bad idea (with several caveats, of course) and the use of Feature Toggles is not always a practical solution to this problem. So get creative and look for ways to not push code to a Production environment until the code is actually meant to be live. This can be accomplished and from my experience it keeps your Production environment more stable.

Story 3: Who's Training Who?

While at one company I saw something I thought was humorous. Maybe it should not have been, but that was my initial reaction. Basically, I was on a Scrum team in an organization that had run several Agile projects with various degrees of success. The latest project by many accounts was a terrible failure in terms of practicing the values and principles of Agile. It was really more of a Water-Scrum-fall project. Several of the Scrum teams had abandoned many of the prescribed practices of Scrum and the idea of continuous improvement (in terms of learning how to build the right software, the right way) had ceased. It seemed like teams were all over the place in terms of what they were doing (some had Scrum meetings, others didn't, some did automated tests, others didn't, etc.).

So it was interesting when one day we received an e-mail offering Scrum training to "show how we do it at XYZ." The e-mail said the class would be "led by a senior member from XYZ." The irony was that when I asked most developers who had been in this organization for a while, they would tell me how things had really degraded in terms of Agile values and principles. I thought to myself, "I wonder who this senior expert is?" and I also thought, "This seems a little like the organization is lying to itself."

Thoughts

Don't get me wrong, I think offering training is great. Increasing employees' knowledge so they can be better at their jobs is always a good thing. But management needs to be honest about what is actually being practiced day to day. As an organization, you want to think you are using Scrum, or Agile more generally, but maybe that is not the reality. This is actually one of my reasons for writing this book: in many organizations, this disconnect exists.

What if the training is a misrepresentation of Agile values and principles? What if those who attend have not been exposed to other Agile training or exposed to Agile in other companies? They might not know to question how things are being done. I am not saying there is a "right" or "wrong," and that is actually one of the great things about Agile; the question "Are we doing Agile right?" is best answered by "Are you following the values?" and "Do what works for your team." That would be fine, but in the organization in Story 3, things were not working.

One good thing about Scrum training, ideally by qualified professionals, is that when developers come back to their teams, organizations, and companies they should have a lot more questions about how things are being done and fresh ideas on what can be improved.

Story 4: Using the "Agile" Excuse

The issue with people in an organization misunderstanding what Agile software development means is that over time, everyone starts buying into the "we're Agile" mentality when the reality could not be farther from the truth. For example, I saw in one organization how such a misunderstanding stops a group from improving. This organization proclaimed to be an "Agile" organization. Within this organization there was a Release Management team that was in charge of making sure all releases went to the Production environment smoothly. While in a meeting with the leader of this group I heard something that really showed me how much people can buy into the idea of being "Agile" when they are far from it. In this particular meeting we were discussing building out a new application and how it would be tested and ultimately released into Production. When we starting talking about how long code changes would take to get into Production, the leader of the Release Management team said "people need to understand that we are Agile and we release code every two weeks to Production."

Thoughts

While it was true that we released code every two weeks, which happened to be the length of our Sprints, it had nothing to do with being Agile. The way a deployable artifact was created in this specific group could not have been further from how you would create an artifact using a CD pipeline. In this group the code was checked into multiple locations, one person controlled who could check in code, and ultimately an artifact was built and deployed to the Production environment. This artifact did not necessarily contain the latest code or reflect what was tested by developers in lower environments. For the most part, it was a manual process and error prone.

The fact that this organization released code every two weeks is not at all specific to Agile software development. Any company can have a two-week software release cycle. But because this group had a mind-set of "we're Agile" and thought their process was fine, I never heard people question things like how the artifacts were being built, why it was a manual process, and why was there a lack of automated testing.

Because the group could simply say "we're Agile" and move on, there was no serious effort to make things better. The danger of buying into the "we're Agile" mentality occurs when Agile software development has been poorly adopted. If people already think they are "Agile" and doing things right, they won't change. If you are in an organization where openness and transparency are not valued, then it makes it harder to face this issue head on. In Story 4, it was very clear that even management had bought into the "we're Agile" mentality, which was unfortunate in the sense that things never improved.

Building Unity

Having a team that can work together toward a common goal is important in any software development methodology, but it is arguably more important in Agile software development: because the team makes a commitment every Sprint, because the teams tend to stay together, and because of the importance of communication on an Agile team. Sometimes team members naturally gel and other times it takes time and effort. The unity comes in meeting the team's Sprint commitment and building working software. This means trusting each person on the team will do his or her part. It means swarming to help each other when someone is blocked. It means doing whatever it takes, as one team, to get the job done.

Real-Life Stories

Story 1: Where Is Everyone?

The best Agile teams I've been on are ones where everyone on the team worked together to achieve a common goal. Every Sprint the team did whatever it took to meet the Sprint commitment. Everyone showed up, day after day, even when some of those days were very long. But on one team I saw the opposite. Granted, each team is different and what works on one team might not work on another team. But on this one team things didn't work all that well. People would completely skip the Daily Stand-up meeting. Some people would completely disappear for days, with no e-mails or any kind of communication. When this became a common occurrence, the cadence of the team really suffered, as you might expect it would. There didn't seem to be a sense of unity. It felt more like ten team members doing their own thing. Some of this occurred because the team lacked a dedicated Scrum Master, and because the team lead was playing that role and he simply did not have the bandwidth to do both roles 100% of the time.

Thoughts

I'm not saying that there is a "right" or "wrong" way for any team to work together, but unity is important on an Agile team. In the case in Story 1, we had a great manager who was a macro manager and very laid back. That was great, but in this case I think some intervention could have helped the team: finding out why team members were not showing up to meetings, impressing upon team members the importance of the Scrum meetings, and impressing upon them the importance of meeting commitments.

The other thing that I've seen help is to have someone dedicated 100% as the Scrum Master. This helps in a few ways: it provides consistency, removes roadblocks, and keeps everyone focused on meeting the Sprint commitment.

Scrum relies heavily on peer pressure. The Daily Stand-up is critical because everyone has to explain what he or she is working on; there is no hiding. You can't claim a great status every day and then not meet your commitment at the end of the Sprint. A lot of pressure is on team members to deliver their share of the point commitment. If a team member is not meeting her commitment, and it is a constant issue, then the other team members should start complaining (either in Retrospective meetings or by voicing concerns privately to the manager).

Story 2: Peer Pressure

One could argue that opposed to Waterfall or RUP, which might have a lot of pressure at the end of the project, Agile has a constant, steady flow of pressure. Instead of being a few months of long hours and stress at the end of a project, it is in two-week bursts. On large projects that last for over six months, this pressure can take its toll. It can lead to things that disrupt the unity (either on a team or across multiple teams).

On one such project I saw how pressure affected people, and how their resulting behavior really killed any sense of unity on the teams. For example, I saw a manager yell at a person in a meeting and storm off. The shock and sense of "what the hell just happened" was palpable in the room. It helped set a negative tone that would last to the end of the project. In another example, one of the analysts on the project yelled at one of the tech leads because something was broken and she wanted it fixed "right now." The bottom line is, treating people as professionals and with respect should be a given.

Thoughts

There's not much to say about Story 2. Things get heated sometimes on projects. But regardless of using Agile or not, treating people with respect is always important. Long after the project ends, you still need to work with these people, so keep that in mind before losing your temper. Reputations will live a lot longer than any project.

In Agile, where communication is so critical, creating any kind of friction between the Scrum team and the business can really be harmful.

Story 3: Burning Out a Team

Another real-life example is having to stay up until 2 a.m. on the last day of the Sprint to close 1 extra point. How does this make sense? This happened on multiple occasions on one project. The manager was adamant that we meet our point commitment. While meeting a commitment is important, his reasons were not particularly valid. His main concern was that our team not "look bad" compared to other teams on the project. I've talked about comparing teams in Chapter 7, Story 2, and why it is a bad idea. Not surprisingly, the amount of turnover on this team was high. By the end of the project, hardly any of the original team members remained; I think 1 original person was left and something like eight people had quit the team. The effect on the team, in terms of a cadence and unity, was very evident.

Thoughts

So is burning out your team for 1 or 2 points advisable (when the Sprint commitment is, say, 15 points)? In my opinion the answer is a resounding "no." In the grand scheme of things, the points will balance out. I am not saying that if a team consistently falls short, there should not be a penalty. I'm talking about when a team that typically meets or exceeds its commitment is forced (and I do mean forced) to work crazy hours just to not miss a point or two in a given Sprint.

I think the key is being realistic: missing a Sprint commitment by a point here and there won't jeopardize a project. Just make it clear to the team members that if they miss a Sprint commitment by 2 points, those 2 points need to be made up before the end of the project. On a sustainment team, this is less of an issue, especially if you are using Kanban. As mentioned in other parts of this book, team members should be allowed to say "OK, we missed the commitment and we will make it up next Sprint."

Story 4: Give Time to Learn New Things

Another way confidence is eroded on teams is when developers don't believe their managers really understand the core principles of Agile. As I've talked about in other chapters, this is not a requirement if other things are in place, like an Agile Coach, a CSM, or training. This was the case on one such team I was on at a retail company. The organization was transitioning to Agile and several members of the leadership had become CSMs. But when talking about things like CI and cross-functional teams, it seemed that these leaders didn't really have much knowledge. That is not necessarily a bad thing unless those are the same people who are supposed to be teaching everyone else about Agile.

People are busy, especially managers of development teams. But if they are leading the transition to Agile, it is crucial that they have some basic under-standing of what Agile is all about. If they don't have the time to learn about Agile, that is fine, but at least bring in an Agile Coach or empower your team members to learn Agile. I've seen that developers who are new to Agile are eager to learn Agile and try new things, so use that energy and enthusiasm to better your team. Give your team members a few hours a week to read articles on Scrum, get a book on starting to use Scrum, find the experts in the field and start following their blogs, and so on. The members of the team can bring this knowledge back to the team and help train others. As the team learns Agile together, team morale will build and the team will understand why unity is important.

Thoughts

I'm not saying that a manager needs to be an expert at Agile or a CSM to man-age Scrum teams. I think it is good, of course, but not required. But if managers are not experienced using Agile, then how can they help guide their teams? How can they help their teams improve and help put teams back on the right path when they start going in the wrong direction? One solution is to have an Agile Coach come in. Another solution is to bring in a few CSMs (if you are following Scrum). Learn from these coaches and CSMs who have experience in the field. Let them help you learn from others' mistakes.

The other thing I think is important is to encourage learning and trying new things. As a manager, demonstrate to your Agile teams that you are taking the time to improve your knowledge of Agile best practices, and so on. Encourage your team members to read articles and books and then bring that knowledge back to the team.

If you are not going to have an Agile Coach or CSM, then offer training to some of the members on the Agile teams. Again, let them bring that knowl-edge back to the team. From there you can try different things and should constantly be improving by reflecting on each Sprint. This way you have a good foundation on which to build the success of your Agile team.

Story 5: Great Teamwork

One of the best examples of unity I've seen occurred while I was on a team where the organization was adopting Agile and the Scrum team was eager to learn Agile. The team I was on consisted of mostly senior developers and only a few had had any exposure to Agile. But the team members were very eager to try Agile. Everyone on the team worked hard to meet each Sprint commitment. We all worked very closely together and would swarm on issues that were blocking anyone on the team.

On this team we also had a concept which seemed pretty unique and was a result of the way teams were structured at this particular organization. Like other organizations I've been at, this organization separated developers by skill sets. We had some developers who were web developers and others who were server-side developers. We paired one web developer and one server-side developer to form a "teamlet." Together a teamlet would work on a User Story. They would create the subtasks, discuss how best to tackle the work, and then work together to get the story completed. These developers counted on one another and that made each not want to let the other developer down. So we had a level of unity at the developer level and then we also had unity on the team level.

Thoughts

The idea of unity across the entire Agile development team is important, but being able to get that at a micro level was something that really worked for that particular team. I find as a developer that focus on collaboration in Agile is one of the most rewarding aspects of using that particular software development methodology. Partnering on User Stories with other developers was very satisfying, and I think it made for a better work environment and better-quality software. This can be accomplished even on teams that don't group developers by skill sets.

Try having multiple developers work on a User Story together. They can create the sub-tasks and divide the work as they best see fit. Contrast that with having a single developer working on a User Story (regardless of size) and see which works better for your team.

Story 6: All Teams Are Not the Same

While not specific to Agile software development, I think having team members who "gel" is more important for Agile teams than for teams using other types of software development methodologies. One of the best Agile teams I've ever worked on was cross-functional. The team members really respected each other, worked really well together, and complemented each other's skill sets. We each knew the others' capabilities, we swarmed on issues, and we were as close to self-organizing as I've seen. This team was very productive, and not surprisingly, the team manager loved to tout our success. As a new project spun up, I was asked to teach other teams "the way we did it." I worked with some other teams to show them how our team worked with the business, how we ran our meetings, and how we were able to have a good, sustainable cadence.

Management thought that they could clone the success of this team simply by forming new teams with the same number of web developers, engineers, and so on, and have the new teams follow the same processes. But it was not too long after this project started that it was clear that it was not that easy. These new teams struggled to work together in this new way. What made it worse was the fact that when these teams did not become as productive as the team I was on, management was not happy. Not surprisingly, these teams felt the pressure and quickly became frustrated because they felt they were unfairly being compared to the other team—and they were right.

Thoughts

At the beginning of the project discussed in Story 6, I must admit even I felt that we could mimic the success of the team I was on. I had read about the "hidden hand of management" on Agile teams and knew that you can't just put any group of people together on an Agile team and expect it to work. It takes time and adjustments (sometimes even of team members) to make a team really good. But after the experience in Story 6, what became clear is that there is a huge difference between learning lessons from other teams vs. reproducing the exact chemistry of a team.

So, the bottom line is to learn lessons from other teams. What have they seen go well? What have been their pain points? But teams don't need to adopt the same culture. As I've discussed in Chapters 7, 8, and 18, comparing team velocities is not a good idea. So don't set up teams for failure by saying "do things like that other team" and just expect to get the same results.

Story 7: Building Team Morale

In comparison to some of the experiences I've discussed in other stories, I've been on teams where the team really knew how to build on its success. On one team in particular, we had a team rule about celebrating success whenever the team would meet or exceed its commitment. When we did not meet our commitment, we really felt bad. We all felt like we needed to try harder the next time. It made the next Sprint that much sweeter when we did meet our commitment. It was not pressure by management but the desire of the team to do our best. We would have our team celebrations during business hours (e.g., leaving early on a Friday and going out to a restaurant, or the like). This not only made the team work harder but kept morale high and showed the team its members were appreciated.

Thoughts

I have been on projects where we only celebrated at the very end of the project, so the way we celebrated in Story 7 was a nice change, and I could see the difference it made. I'm not saying that you need to celebrate every time the team meets or exceeds its commitment, but the point is to celebrate the team's success. The show of appreciation can go a long way. Again, it does not have to be all the time, but make sure it is tied to a success.

Build on your success. When something goes well (whether it is some process that made a big difference or some architectural issue the team overcame, etc.), build upon that success. Take the energy from that success and use it to motivate the team.

The aforementioned items are not specific to the Agile software development methodology. But I think they are more important when using Agile because the team is always delivering and there is no real "end," as you might have on a traditional project.

Keeping Engaged

One of the great things about Agile is that teams tend to stay together. This is key because the longer a team stays together, the better its members can estimate work, the better its velocity becomes, and the better team members work together. This, of course, is not always the case, but I've seen it occur on most teams. However, with keeping developers on the same team and working on the same product for long periods of time, keeping developers engaged is an issue. By engaged I don't just mean in terms of having enough work to keep busy but also in terms of the type of work so they are happy.

Real-Life Stories

Story 1: Keeping It Fresh

On my first few Agile teams it was clear that having a team stay together for multiple projects really did increase velocity. The team became a well-oiled machine over time. On one Scrum team we had been together for about a year and a half and worked pretty much on the same codebase (similar to the Micro Service Architecture structure that other companies have adopted). After a while, I found this boring because there was little challenge to the day-to-day work (in terms of both domain knowledge and technical skills). Eventually I left the team so that I could find more challenging work.

Thoughts

I realize that my choice to leave the team, mentioned in Story 1, was a very individual one. For some developers the idea of staying on a team where they know the code inside and out would be ideal. But for other developers, it can get old after a while.

However, there are ways to keep developers engaged and challenged on Agile teams that work on the same product. One way is to give developers "hack hours" every week so they can work on projects they are interested in. These projects can be focused on reducing development pain points or just learning some new technology.

Another approach that I've seen work well is to have team members rotate certain roles on the team. Some teams, for example, rotate the Scrum Master role. This can break up the monotony, create an opportunity for growth, and make team members feel more fulfilled.

Story 2: A Lot of Free Time

When developers are not challenged at work, it can lead to some very interesting situations. Although such a situation is not specific to those working in Agile software development, I think in Agile it should be easier to identify when this is happening (Daily Stand-ups, point commitments, etc.). On one Scrum team I was on, I saw that even with Daily Stand-up meetings and other processes, several developers were not being challenged by the work our team was doing. In fact, several developers would openly work on non-company-related development during the day. I am not talking about approved "hack days" or anything like that. They were working on things related to their own outside businesses. I actually saw one developer get swamped with work while two other developers were working on non-work-related development. I thought to myself, "how is no one at the management level noticing this?"

Thoughts

In Story 2, the main issue was a lack of transparency. If developers would say "I'll have those User Stories done in one week" and the Sprint is two weeks, then it should be obvious they have bandwidth to work on other things (defects, improvements, etc.). As members of a Scrum team, there is an expectation that we are transparent in Sprint Planning and the Daily Stand-up meetings.

One-on-one meetings can go a long way toward helping you to know if developers are being challenged or losing interest. I've always found these types of meetings to be very useful. It's an excellent chance for managers and developers to touch base. It's a chance for managers to ask if developers are happy or are looking to try something new. This is not Agile specific, but it is one way for managers to have insight into what is happening on their Agile teams. In general, teams I've been on that had one-on-one meetings seemed to have happier developers; of course, this is just empirical data.

It should go without saying that team members should be helping each other to complete the work for the Sprint. One way to make sure this is happening is for developers to ask for help in the Daily Stand-up meeting. This forces members of the team to justify why they can't assist.

Story 3: Avoid Pigeonholing

Sometimes on Scrum teams developers can get pigeonholed. For example, I have been on teams where someone becomes the dedicated QA person. On one team I saw a QA engineer get pigeonholed where he became the only person on the team to run the Automation test suite we had for the codebase. This particular team was practicing BDD and we had a substantial set of automated functional tests. This one person would run the tests every day and report the failed tests. In addition to running the automated functional tests, he would also maintain the functional environment (we were using Selenium Grid and testing across multiple browsers). Over time, this became a very monotonous task.

Not surprisingly, this individual became pretty bored. For some reason our manager only wanted this person to focus on this one area of the project. This QA engineer was very talented and could have contributed to other areas of the project (writing tests, fixing defects, etc.). It was unfortunate because this individual had a lot of experience that could have benefited the project.

Thoughts

Not only does pigeonholing people on a cross-functional Scrum team hurt those individuals, but it is bad for the team and company. It is bad for the individual because he never gets a chance to grow in his career. It is bad for the team and company because having a single point of failure is never good.

One way to overcome this pigeonholing is to rotate roles on a team. I am talking about on cross-functional teams where people are separated by skill sets. I know in some companies "everyone plays every role" on the Agile team, so rotating roles does not apply. You can also rotate the Scrum Master role if you are using Scrum.

Depending on the way your teams are structured, maybe it is possible to rotate developers between teams. For example, I have seen sustainment teams using Kanban and project teams using Scrum and every other month or so developers are swapped between these teams. If your teams are following a model where your teams own a complete Service or vertical (UI to Service for a functional area in an application) and handle both product defects and project work, then you can try rotating developers between working on defect and project work every few Sprints. Again, it depends on the structure of your teams and the dynamics, but I think rotating developers in and out of production defect type of work is a good idea because it can help developers write better code (because they know what it means to support code in a Production environment).

Fundamental Misunderstandings

In an organization that is using Agile software development, can managers with no Agile experience or training be effective? Should they have some basic understanding so that they can guide Agile teams in the right direction? Or, does it matter if the team is self-organizing? Can a lack of understanding about Agile software development by managers harm Agile teams? Some of the best Agile projects I have been involved in were ones where the managers spent a lot of time learning Agile best practices and what works for other companies running Agile projects. On projects where this was not the case, we tended to have a lot of issues.

Real-Life Stories

Story 1: Artificial Limits

While on a Scrum team I saw an example of what happens when managers put aside Agile values and principles that they either don't understand or don't like. On this specific Scrum team, instead of the team determining what it would take on in a given Sprint, the manager had a rule of each developer only taking on 3 points. This rule had been in place before I joined the team, so one day I asked, "Where does the 3-points-per-developer rule come from?" I was told that it was based on historic data.

But while on this team, I saw that some developers could easily do 6 or even 9 points in a given Sprint. Even faced with that fact, the manager did not want to change the "3-points-per-developer" rule. If you did more than 3 points during a Sprint you were almost seen as rocking the boat.

So, as you might imagine, User Stories that were over 3 points would get split into smaller User Stories that were 3 points or less. The problem is that splitting User Stories this way often meant that at the end of the Sprint, we could only demo partial functionality. This was not even close to being a shippable product (I discuss that specific issue and how it relates to transparency in Chapters 4 and 9).

Thoughts

I think there are many ways to track a team's productivity in terms of how many points are closed per developer per Sprint. There is nothing wrong with understanding, for example, that each developer on a team can close an average of 5 points in a Sprint. That kind of data is great for Program Managers to understand how a project is trending and to plan capacity. But the real measure, in terms of Agile, for understanding how a team is performing should be its velocity.

The other issue with the situation in Story 1 was a manager being the one to dictate how many points the team could commit to per Sprint. The Sprint commitment should be made by the team, not the manager. Also, by having a flat number of points per developer, the team's velocity will always be the same. If the expectations from the manager are that the team will always close X points in a Sprint, then what is the motivation for the team to improve its velocity?

So the bottom line is that the members of a Scrum team should be the ones making the Sprint commitment, not someone outside the Scrum team ("chickens" in Scrum). The team has to do the work and knows what its members are capable of, so let them make the commitment. If they make the commitment, they will feel more responsible for meeting the commitment.

Story 2: Merging of Roles

In one organization I was a team lead for a Scrum team. In this particular organization, three roles were blended into one. The team lead was also the technical lead and the Scrum Master. In my case, I played these three roles and also spent about 50% of my time doing development. This is a lot of work for one person, but I had had several years of experience with Agile projects at this point, so that really helped. I had seen many different things that worked and that didn't work.

However, in other cases I've seen that the person playing the Scrum Master role did not have much experience. That is not necessarily a problem, but when you combine being a Scrum Master with the other roles I mentioned, it can be difficult. I saw this first-hand on one Scrum team where the team lead was playing the Scrum Master role but did not have adequate time to spend on being an effective Scrum Master. Being a good Scrum Master is not easy. It takes a lot of time and effort. It takes finding creative solutions to issues. On the team I just, the thought was that being the Scrum Master was something anyone could do and should not be a full-time role. However, that is not what I've seen in my experience on several Scrum teams; it can easily be a full-time job.

Thoughts

One thing I've seen work well is to have team members take turns being the Scrum Master. There is no set rotation, but I've seen rotating the role every Sprint work pretty well. During the time that a person is the Scrum Master, he or she is dedicated 100% to that role. He or she does not commit to points for that Sprint or take on additional work. At the end of the Sprint, the role transitions to the next person. If switching the Scrum Master every Sprint creates too many handoffs or things falling between the cracks, then try rotating the position on a different frequency.

Bring in a CSM to help the team. Have the CSM train others to be a good Scrum Master. Once people are trained, keep one person dedicated to being the Scrum Master for the team. An Agile Coach can help in a similar way.

Story 3: Agile Smells

There are a lot of things that I have begun to see as red flags when working on an Agile project or team. For example, one team lead used to say, "It is time for Scrum." I used to think to myself, "Scrum is not a specific meeting." I've heard it called "Daily Scrum" or more generally "Daily Stand-up meeting." Of course, this is a nit-picky thing, but combined with other things it becomes a red flag.

Another example was when a manager said "one point is 20 hours" when our team was estimating User Stories for the Product Backlog. I asked "why are we even using points if we are translating them directly to hours anyway?" I was more or less told that "in Agile you have to use points for User Stories." So we basically did all estimates in points but discussed points in terms of hours. It was a strange exercise to say the least.

In another example, the manager of the team was the one doing the estimations for the User Stories, not the team members. He said he did the t-shirt sizing and would give those estimates back to the business. Then the team would be left doing the work and having to hit the dates based on the manager's estimates.

Thoughts

I'm not saying that the items mentioned in Story 3 are necessarily wrong, but I am saying that in an organization that proclaims to be Agile, these are red flags. Hearing and seeing things like the items mentioned have taught me to set expectations. They show the amount of experience groups or individuals have with Agile. It shows their understanding of fundamental Agile concepts.

I mention some of these red flags in Chapter 9. As mentioned in that chapter, the main point is that hearing and seeing things like I describe in Story 3 can erode the confidence developers have in leadership.

The point is, when I've seen fundamental misunderstandings of Agile values and practices, it always worries me a little. But there is a positive side as well. The positive side is that there is an opportunity to teach people and share Agile experiences. By sharing our knowledge, as long as the organization and management are open to learning, we all grow and learn how Agile can make software development better.

Story 4: Going Through the Motions

One Scrum team that I was on had a very interesting way to conduct the Daily Stand-up meeting. This team was at a very successful electronics company with a lot of really smart engineers. Every morning we would head into the conference room. We would turn on the TV and sit around the conference table, someone would connect her laptop, and then she would open a browser. Then she would open a wiki page which had a few things on it: date, attendees, and notes for each attendee. The manager would typically copy the previous days "status" wiki page and clear out all the sections. This would eat up about the first five minutes of the meeting. Then the manager would proceed to go around the table and ask what each person had done the prior day. The next day we would repeat this process.

Thoughts

In Story 4, there is nothing wrong with what this team was doing. As a matter of fact, it was one of the most casual meetings I had ever seen. The team was doing what worked for them, and that is great. My only issue occurs when a team says it is practicing Scrum but then does things that are contrary to what Scrum prescribes. In this case, the Daily Stand-up meeting was anything but a stand-up meeting, and it did not provide the value that it should. Again, I am not saying the process the team used was bad; it just was not typical for a Scrum team.

Story 5: What Are We Building?

Considering that the output of Agile software development is quality, working software that delivers business value, it is curious when I have seen leadership on Agile projects not grasp that concept. For example, I'm a big fan of the idea of "building software right" and "building the right software." I don't recall where I first was introduced to this way of looking at software development, but I believe it was related to BDD. What it basically says is that you can build software the right way (in terms of quality, etc.) but that does not mean it is the right software if it does not behave as expected. You need to do both in order to both provide business value now and create quality software that is maintainable in the future. I tried to discuss this with a manager one time but he didn't care about this concept. He was simply more interested in getting code pushed through the pipeline.

Thoughts

Although not everyone on Agile projects might have heard of these particular quotes in Story 5, I would think people would be curious about the ideas. If nothing else, developers and anyone involved in an Agile project should understand the importance of building the right software and building it the right way.

Story 6: Things Are Not Always Interchangeable

A fundamental principle of Agile is understanding that *what* is delivered to the business every Sprint is more important than just delivering User Stories. But on one Scrum team there was a mentality that the amount of points completed in a Sprint was the most important measure. During a Daily Stand-up meeting we were discussing that some of the User Stories we committed to might be in jeopardy and we were told that "as long as we close 20 points this Sprint, it doesn't matter which User Stories constitute those 20 points."

To be fair, part of this mentality was due to the fact that this group was doing more Water-Scrum-fall, even though they thought they were doing pure Scrum. But with that aside, I was still surprised that the idea that we build the Sprint Backlog based on what Product Owner sees as the most valuable was lost on some people. In other words, there was a mind-set that all User Stories are equal.

Thoughts

One of the Agile values is the early and continuous delivery of valuable software—which to me means we not only deliver value but also quality software. So even if you are following Water-Scrum-fall, this should still apply. Forget the misunderstanding of thinking all User Stories are equal and planning to deliver all the features by the end of the project, why would you not work on the most valuable features first? What if, as often happens, the project hits crunch time toward the end and the quality goes out the window? Will the most valuable features now be the worst implemented ones and least tested ones? How can that be a good thing?

So I think whether you are following Scrum or another form of Agile, or Water-Scrum-fall, the Product Owner should be prioritizing what the team works on each Sprint. The work delivered by the team should always be providing value to the business.

Story 7: Cliff Dives

I've been on several teams that had a nice burn-down chart Sprint after Sprint. I've also been on teams that had "cliff dive" burn-down charts. Based on my experience, I can say it definitely matters. In the cliff dive Sprints, people worked long hours at the end of the Sprint, and on teams with QA members, they would get overwhelmed the last few days of the Sprint. I was on one team, though, that accepted cliff dives as a normal circumstance. On this team we had a rule that each developer does 2 points per Sprint and almost all the estimated stories were 2 points. So basically all the developers would finish their development at the end of the Sprint. This meant our QA engineer would become overloaded the last few days. This was not very fair to the QA engineer. Not surprisingly, the burn-down chart always looked like a cliff dive at the end of the Sprint. This is far from what would be a "nice burn-down chart" in Scrum, where you have a steady burn starting at the beginning at the Sprint and the burn-down line stays close to the trend line.

Thoughts

I think a better way to work is to be delivering stories to be tested through-out the Sprint, every few days—basically, a nice steady stream of work that moves across the task board as the Sprint moves along. You can imagine on day 1 that all the stories are in the "not started" column. Then maybe on day 3 you have some stories in the "not started" column and a few in the "in progress" column. Then in the next few days a few stories end up in the "closed" column and the rest of the "not started" stories make their way across the board throughout the Sprint. The burn-down chart would look like a nice steady burn of points. It means that everyone on the team is busy and there is not a pile of work thrown on the QA people at the end of the Sprint. I've seen this work both on Scrum teams and on teams using Kanban. The key is to not say developers can only do X points per Sprint but, rather, to build the Sprint Backlog based on the team's past velocity and current capacity. As developers finish their stories, they grab the next "not started" story from the Story Backlog. You can then put stories of all sizes in the backlog and you will be delivering stories throughout the Sprint.

Of course, there are always unforeseen blockers that might cause stories to not close until the end of the Sprint. The occasional cliff dive is bound to happen. I am not saying that it will never happen; rather, I'm saying that cliff dives should not be the norm and frequent cliff diving is a red flag. So look at your processes and determine why the cliff dives are happening and find ways to avoid them.

Story 8: Things Always Breaking

While on one team I experienced what happens when there is a lack of under-standing about Agile principles, specifically around giving people the environment and support they need to be successful. This was a Scrum team that was in an organization that claimed to be "Agile." But as a developer who has worked on a lot of teams at several companies, this was probably the first time that I felt very hesitant about making code changes. This is because the environment was very unstable, from both an infrastructure and a support standpoint.

We had a set of REST APIs (application programming interfaces) and there were several issues, like no real versioning, no real integration tests, and a lack of unit-level tests. These things, coupled with the complexity of the code, made adding new functionality a very difficult endeavor. It was difficult in the sense that for every new feature added, we would see about three defects created in existing functionality. The new functionality would work according to the acceptance criteria, but there were side effects on the UI or other services that would not get uncovered until later in the development process.

To make matters worse, all code developed during a Sprint, even though potentially not complete in terms of being fully integration tested, was deployed to the Production environment. There was a notion that this was OK because we were using Feature Toggles or had "if/else" logic in the code. But the evidence was clear: this approach did not work for this particular organization.

Thoughts

The work environment described in Story 8 was incredibly stressful. I don't mean stressful in the sense of deadlines or constant changes to requirements but because, as a developer, you never felt confident (other than additive changes) that something wasn't broken somewhere else and you hadn't realized it. Then, all of a sudden, someone would come over and say "Oh crap! We broke something in Production." It was a constant firefighting environment.

Many factors can lead to the type of development environment described in Story 8. In this case, a big part of the stressful environment was a lack of automated functional tests and the fact that we had somewhere around 17 services that comprised the REST API. Very few of the developers knew how all these services integrated. At the time of writing this book, the jury is still out on Micro-Service Architectures (MSAs). After seeing how some organizations approach MSAs, I am now more in the camp of starting with larger applications and splitting them later as needed. But even with MSAs, the key is to have automated tests (unit, functional, and integration tests). Only with a high level of automated tests can you really trust CI and rely less on manual testing.

In Story 8, management knew about this constant firefighting, but it was accepted as the "norm," and a mentality of "it is what it is" was prevalent. It was unfortunate because things could have been improved by adding more automated tests and with more knowledge sharing across teams. With no management support, and developers always putting out fires, there was no time to really fix the underlying problems.

Story 9: Diminishing Returns

On several teams I've had managers talk about "swarming to close points." What they meant was simply to have more developers work on a single User Story so it could be closed more quickly—which usually made the work go slower because developers had to merge changes, have more meetings, and so on. There really can be too many cooks in the kitchen. I am not saying that having multiple developers work on the same User Story is a bad thing. To the contrary, I think having multiple developers work on one story can make a lot of sense if the work can be divided in a logical way.

Thoughts

When I've seen swarming done as in Story 9, it seemed like a misunderstanding of what swarming really means. I believe swarming means that a team works together to get past a specific problem or impediment. So if one person is stuck on something, other members of the team stop and together they swarm on the impediment until the original team member is unblocked. There are several definitions of swarming, so this is just my take on it.

Story 10: Something Is Missing

At one retail company I saw how hard it is to adopt Agile when managers do not understand some of the basic concepts. For instance, the particular application my team worked on had no unit tests and when I raised this as a concern the manager was a bit confused about why that would be an issue. We had a conversation that went something like the following:

> Me: "Are we going to have CI at some point?"
>
> Technical Manager: "Yes, eventually we would like to get a CI pipeline up and running."
>
> Me: "So, I am noticing a lack of unit-level tests in the codebase."
>
> Technical Manager: "Really? Why is that an issue?"
>
> Me: "Well, in order to have Continuous Integration, you need tests that can be run against the codebase when developers check in code to detect when the codebase has been broken."
>
> Technical Manager: "Makes sense."

Thoughts

It was really eye opening to have the conversation shown in Story 10. In this particular case, there were several senior developers on the team, but still unit testing seemed to not be a major concern.

Having unit tests is crucial for CI to be of value. The purpose of integrating your code often is to know that you have not broken anything and you need tests in order to determine that. Unit tests are also critical so that developers can feel safe when refactoring code. CI is such a critical part of Agile and allows teams to delivery early and often. Anyone on an Agile team should have a good grasp of CI, if not CD.

Story 11: Ineffective Demo Meetings

One of the things I like about Scrum is the Demo meeting. This meeting gives the Product Owner a chance to accept the work that the team did during the Sprint. Only when the Product Owner has accepted the work can the team collect the points for the work and close the User Stories. If the Product Owner does not accept some of the work, then those User Stories are revisited in the next Sprint.

But I've seen Agile projects where this was not the case. I was on one project where we collected the points and closed the User Stories before the Demo meeting. Worse was the fact that on this particular project we had combined Demo meetings. Each Scrum team only had a few minutes to demonstrate the User Stories they worked on during the Sprint. There was hardly enough time to show the User Stories we had worked on. There was very little time to test all the scenarios and truly allow the Product Owner to ask questions. Teams rushed to demo their User Stories and skimmed over the details.

Thoughts

The way the Demo meetings were run in Story 11 was not fair to the Scrum teams doing the work, and was also not fair to the Product Owner. Adequate time was not given to truly look at what was being delivered in the Sprint. Combining a Demo meeting with several teams, because it was easier to have just a single meeting, had consequences. For one, many people stopped showing up to the Demo meeting because they felt it was not adding any value. Second, many defects were found later when the Product Owner really had a chance to test the new features. Finally, it tended to compare teams in terms of what was done during that Sprint, and in my opinion, it is not a good practice to compare team's velocities.

A better approach, and one I have seen work well on other projects, is to have smaller Demo meetings with just the team doing the work and the Product Owner. This meeting should be a real conversation about what was built and allow the Product Owner to ask questions. Only when the Product Owner is satisfied can the team collect the points. This is like other areas in life where you only get paid after doing the work.

Challenges with Estimations

One of the biggest challenges teams have when adopting Agile is the idea of estimating work. When you are used to estimating everything in hours, it is difficult to start estimating work in terms of points or relative sizing. It takes time to adjust to this new way of estimating work. The urge to spend a lot of time getting into every detail of a piece of work before committing to an estimate is sometimes hard to resist. The more estimating a team does, the less team members will think in terms of time and the more they will think in terms of points. The key is to understand why Agile uses points and to understand what goes into determining the points on a User Story.

Real-Life Stories

Story 1: Estimation Overkill

The idea of using relative sizing to estimate User Stories is something I've seen work pretty well. The idea of creating a "golden story" and then measuring other stories against it can work really well. But this takes a certain level of comfort with not knowing all the details of a User Story.

While on a Scrum team I saw how difficult this can be. This particular team wanted to have an extremely high level of confidence in the estimates. Even though they thought they were a Scrum team, the five-hour marathon meetings we had talking about User Stories to just get an estimate said we were far from Scrum. After hours and hours of talking about all the "what if" dependencies and possible implementations, I didn't find that our estimates were any better than if we just did relative sizing.

Thoughts

For organizations that are used to giving estimates in units of time (typically hours), it is hard to adjust to using story points. Further, for teams that are used to getting very detailed in order to get a "level of effort," it is hard to accept that you can't predict everything.

As I mentioned, the estimates in Story 1 took about a week to come up with and I'm not convinced that the estimates were better than using relative sizing. I've seen on other teams where we did relative sizing and over time we got better and better at estimating. That is why I like the concept of two rounds of estimating in Scrum. The first estimate occurs when the stories are put into the Product Backlog. The second estimate, or re-estimate, occurs during the Sprint Planning meeting when the team learns more about the User Story. In Scrum it is important to always keep three things in mind when estimating a User Story: risk, complexity, and effort. I've found that keeping these things in mind when going through the estimation process, and having a golden User Story, helps to keep estimates consistent.

I think it takes time for an Agile team to become comfortable with the idea that you don't need to know every detail when first estimating a story. You obviously need to understand enough to estimate it, but not every little detail and not to the level of designing solutions. Again, you'll have another chance to estimate the story before committing to it for a Sprint. In the end, I think the amount of User Stories that go up in number of points and those that go down in number of points ends up being a wash over the long run.

Story 2: Who Estimated This?

One of the things I've enjoyed while being on Agile teams is the idea that the team gets to estimate the work. This is only fair seeing that team members are the ones who have to do the work. But while on an e-commerce team I saw something that was the exact opposite of a team doing the estimates. This team was in an organization that was adopting Agile software development. Only a few developers had had experience working on Agile teams at other companies. The manager of the team had some experience but hadn't been using Agile recently.

The manager would work with the business to determine what work would go into a release. The manager would do t-shirt sizing of what the organization was calling User Stories. Then the team was expected to deliver everything that the manager promised. Not surprisingly, the team felt a little upset when the manager overcommitted the team.

For some of the developers like me, who had been on several Agile teams, this seemed very strange and definitely not what you would see on a typical Scrum team. The team should have been doing the estimates, not the manager.

Thoughts

As I mentioned in Story 2, one of the things I like most about working on Agile teams, specifically Scrum teams, is that the team gets to estimate the work. It is only fair that the team doing the work gets a chance to estimate the work. If not, the idea of velocity and letting the team self-organize is not going to work.

The key is to not change the measure of a point over time. It is tempting to change the meaning of a point over time as a team gets better and knows more about the space its members are working in. For example, you may have estimated a story as 3 points and then, when you work on it months later, you may say, "We can do that faster now, so let's make it 2 points." But that is dangerous because it is going to skew the velocity of the team. The same is true if you start changing the definition of "done done." You might be tempted to change the rules for "done done" over time, but again, that can skew the velocity because now the things needed to close a 3-point story are not the same as they used to be. It is important to keep the measure the same over time using a "golden story" and a consistent definition for your "Steps to Doneness."

Story 3: Excuse for Poor Estimating

One thing that I have seen Agile teams do when writing User Stories is to add a "technical assumptions" section to the story. The team puts all its technical assumptions in this section, things like "logging framework already exists" or "database is already designed." When the team works on the story during a Sprint and finds that one of the assumptions is not true, it has the opportunity to increase the point value on the story or create a separate story to handle the "unanticipated" work. On one team, though, I saw this lead to poor estimating because the team knew it could use these "technical assumptions" as a way to increase the points on a story later.

Thoughts

Historically I've been a proponent of having this "technical assumptions" section on User Stories. I've been on several Agile projects where we used such a section with great success. But I've come to question this approach after the experience with the team I mentioned in the Story 3.

Is it really just a way for the team to make up for bad estimating or to artificially increase its velocity? When we estimate stories, especially when using t-shirt or relative sizing, we don't know every little detail, and isn't the estimate based on effort, complexity, and risk? Without this "technical assumptions" section, if you hit something unexpected while working on a User Story, it becomes blocked and that impediment will need to be removed; this is what I would call the typical workflow for a Scrum team. I think having these "technical assumptions" can lead to poor estimating because the team knows it has a way to change the point value during the Sprint. For me, the jury is still out on this approach, but I would lean toward not using it as part of your estimating process.

Story 4: Another Reason to Use Points

Learning to measure work using story points can be difficult. I've been in organizations that are trying to adopt Agile but are stuck in a mentality of measuring work in time. For example, I was on a project where we were supposedly using Scrum, but yet we still measured our work in hours. Instead of having a golden story and thinking about complexity, effort, and risk when estimating a story, we would discuss how many hours the User Story would take a "typical" developer. When discussing how many hours a User Story would take, we would talk about things like unit testing, and so on. In this particular organization we still had Project Managers. Technically there is nothing wrong with that, and they can coexist with Agile. The problem was that when a project started to slip, the Project Managers saw that unit testing was a significant part of the estimate and deemed it "nonessential" for the project. Regardless of whether this particular project was Agile or not, sacrificing unit tests to meet a deadline is usually a short-sighted decision.

Thoughts

There are many things that were wrong with that mentality of cutting unit tests on the project mentioned in Story 4. But for the purposes of this discussion, I will focus on why using story points is a better approach than using hours.

I think if you are using story points it is much harder for project managers to think about cutting quality. If a story is estimated using points, their only option is to remove scope from the User Story or split the User Story into several stories and maybe move some of them to a future phase.

Let's look at an example. Let's say you have a User Story with a point value of 5. Then the project starts to slip and the Project Manager wants start shaving time off the project. When a User Story is about functionality and estimated as 5 points, the option to remove time is gone. The only option is to either remove functionality from the User Story or split the User Story into several User Stories. So let's say they split the User Story into two stories (one story being 2 points and the other story being 3 points). So now the Product Owner decides the 3-point story is more important, so it stays in the Product Backlog. The 2-point story gets moved to an unscheduled application version or something similar depending on your issue tracking system. From an Agile standpoint, this is a much better way to handle change. Instead of sacrificing quality, you shift scope.

Story 4 provides a simple example, but I think it is just one reason why using story points is better than estimating using time. There are many articles and resources that discuss other reasons why story points were introduced in the first place, so I would recommend doing further reading to understand why story points are important.

Story 5: Right Flavor of Agile

While on an e-commerce team at a decent-sized company in the retail industry I saw how picking the right flavor of Agile really matters. This team was in an organization that was just starting to adopt Agile software development. The manager had some experience with Agile and was a CSM.

As we started to adopt the Agile software development methodology, the decision was made that Scrum would be the best fit. However, this decision did not work particularly well because this team was doing mostly Production support and had constant fly-ins (defects and new features). But because the manager had already committed the team to other things in the current release of the application, the team sometimes had to work extra hours to get everything done.

Thoughts

Over time, the various flavors of Agile have evolved. Using the right flavor of Agile to suit your particular needs is important. I've seen where people go to Scrum certification training and think that they "must" use Scrum. So, like the team in Story 5, they try to fit their teams into the Scrum model when it might not be the right fit. While on the team in Story 5, I recommended that we shift to using Kanban.

I had also read several articles on how teams at other companies were using Agile on Production support teams, and it was clear that many companies were struggling with how to use Agile in such an environment. I found a really good article about how one company handles this problem (Use of Kanban in the Operations Team at Spotify, by Michael Prokop and Mattias Jansson, which you can find here: http://www.infoq.com/articles/kanban-operations-spotify). The company uses a "goalkeeper" to manage fly-ins and prioritize work. Any person on the team could play the role of "goalkeeper," and it was not just one person who had this responsibility every Sprint. I was able to convince my manager to try this approach. It definitely helped our team to better handle the fly-in defects. It was clear that using Kanban, combined with the "goalkeeper" approach, was a much better fit for this team than Scrum.

CHAPTER

14

Transparency

The importance of transparency in Agile software development cannot be overstated. In some organizations it is not easy to be transparent and open. There is a lot of pressure to say what the business wants to hear. But I believe, in the long run, that a lack of transparency hurts an Agile team, the project, and the company. Having seen first-hand organizations that claim they want "openness" but then don't listen or, worse, punish those who are open, I can say that true transparency is not easy. But it is critical to the success of Agile software development and worth the effort.

Real-Life Stories

Story 1: Lack of Commitment

I was fortunate enough to work on an amazing project at a major entertainment company. The project would allow users to have highly customized vacations. It was truly going to be a game changer in this specific industry. Soon after joining this team, I attended my first Sprint Planning meeting. During the meeting I noticed something odd. The team's true velocity was, let's say, 30 points, but they would only commit to around 20 points. They would then find a few more stories and put them in the next Sprint. These additional stories were "a stretch goal." But they knew their velocity was much higher than what they were committing to. This seemed very wrong to me. It was a total lack of transparency and honesty.

Not surprisingly, the team would typically finish the stories in the current Sprint and then work on a few more stories from the next Sprint that they had put aside. For the most part, this was a management decision because management did not trust the team to meet their velocity in a consistent fashion. This led to a lack of transparency with the business, and normal tools like burn-down charts could not be trusted. Also, it did not make the team feel very good because team members knew they were not being honest with the business.

Thoughts

Use the velocity of the team to measure how much work can be done in a given Sprint. Then, based on capacity, commit to what you know your team can complete during that Sprint.

Be honest about the team's velocity and don't give into political games about trying "to look good" on some presentation slide. This type of misrepresentation does not benefit anyone in the long run.

Use burn-down charts to be honest about how the team is performing in a given Sprint. A burn-down chart tells the true story of how the team is performing. Some teams also use a burn-up chart for this purpose. If you cliff dive at the end of the Sprint, that's not the greatest, but at least you are being honest with the Product Owner in terms of what happened. If you are not going to make the Sprint commitment, at least that will be more obvious during the Sprint (i.e., the burn-down will show that the team is not closing enough points each day and is at risk of either cliff diving or not meeting the commitment). The point is that the team is being completely transparent.

Using the raw data and not hiding anything from the business frees an Agile team. Kent Beck has an excellent quote in one of his presentations about what he calls "schedule chicken." He tells a story about people around the table during a typical project meeting and the project manager who is walking around and asking each team how things are going. Everyone wants to put on a good face and say "umm, yeah we are on schedule," even when he is not. Now each person has to sit there and know that he might be caught it a lie later. It is better to just be honest and say "well, we are about two Sprints behind." Done. Now there is nothing to hide and you can move on and deal with the reality of the situation you are faced with.

Let the quality of the team's work speak for itself. Have a consistent velocity, deliver software without defects, deliver business value, and adapt to what the business needs.

Story 2: Misleading Numbers

I was on a large multiyear project with dozens of Scrum teams. There was a lot of pressure on the teams to use BDD. Unfortunately, many of the teams were new to BDD and the infrastructure needed to scale automated functional tests was not in place. We had dashboards displayed on large flat-screen TVs in various development areas. It showed the automated functional test results for each team, which were aligned with functional verticals. These tests were run as part of the CI pipeline. These information radiators were supposed to alert teams to broken builds.

Over time, some teams, with their manager's knowledge, started to game the system. They would put "skip" meta tags in the tests when the tests would fail. Then they showed as green on the dashboard monitors around the development area. But this was completely misleading and produced a false sense of confidence in the quality of the application. Over time, it became a bit of joke among developers. Upper management was just glad to see green builds in CI. Worse yet, as I talked about in Chapter 7, the automated functional tests were eventually completely turned off.

Thoughts

One of the Agile principles is delivering quality software early and often that provides value to the business. But in order to know that you are building quality software and to have a high level of confidence in your software, you need to be open about the amount of testing that is being done. It is crucial, for the sake of building trust with the business, to be open about the quality of the software you are building. If not, the business will eventually find out anyway due to high defect counts and poor user experiences, and ultimately it will hurt the name of the company.

Story 3: Caving into Pressure

The question of pressure on team members in a cross-functional team was something I had been curious about since the first Agile project I had been on. During my first few Agile projects, I did not see pressure play a big part and did not see it lead to developers lowering their standards. Nor did I see pressure get to other team members, like the QA member of the team, to the point where they lowered their standards. Each person on the team pushed back whenever there was pressure to get them to accept software that was below our standards.

Then, on one project, I saw the pressure of meeting Sprint commitments completely erode the professionalism of some team members. It happened at the end of the Sprint, when the pressure on the QA engineer to close stories was very high. In this case, the team collected points when the story was passed by our QA engineer, not after the Product Owner accepted the features during the demo meeting. Often when the QA engineer would find a defect, there would be pressure to call it a "tech debt item" or say something like "we will fix that in the next Sprint." This also happened to the Product Owner. The Product Owner had the ultimate signoff on a User Story and also felt pressure to ignore certain things for the benefit of the team. There was a mentality of "the team worked really hard, so we can ignore this defect for now." I often questioned this mentality and pushed for a zero-defect policy, but I was overruled. Worse, on this particular project, there was a measure of success that said if we did not have severity 1 or 2 defects, then the project could go live. So what happened? Defects slowly but surely went from severity 2 to a 3 or 4.

The pressure on teams was high to portray the right picture, and people's standards and professionalism started to slip. There was a total lack of transparency to the business in terms of what was being delivered and the quality of the application.

Thoughts

When on a cross-functional team there can be a lot of pressure to close stories so the team can meet its Sprint commitment. But it is critical to the success of the team, the project, and the spirit of being transparent to be open about what the team is delivering. Each person on the team is a professional, and if he or she were in an environment that had clear boundaries between disciplines, I believe he or she would be less susceptible to caving in to peer pressure. Yes, even professionals on an Agile team can feel peer pressure.

So, what can be done to prevent this? I think one important thing is to have clear "Steps to Doneness." In your "Steps to Doneness," state that the User Story can only be closed if, for example, it has no defects (even visual). Of course, these rules are up to your team and there is no right answer. Clearly state that the team values openness and what the standards are for closing a story/feature. Then people can point to these team rules and standards. Of course, this is only as valuable as the team that adheres to rules. Team members need to support each other and hold each other to the highest standards.

At the end of the day we all have bosses, so it is crucial that management respect and support the values of the team. With these values in place, and knowing they are supported by their manager, team members can feel good about not compromising. They can feel good knowing that they are being completely open with their business partners. In my opinion, this is a much better way to work and removes a lot of stress.

Specifications and Testing

Having good User Stories, acceptance criteria, and functional tests are all critical to being successful in Agile software development. The value of good acceptance criteria and using BDD to drive your design is something that Agile teams need to understand. The importance of investing in automated functional tests is also something that needs to be understood and invested in. Often teams waste a lot of time on writing documents in multiple places and keeping them synchronized. Quickly these get outdated and very rarely reflect what the software is actually doing. I think a better approach is to have what Gojko Adzic calls "living documentation."

Real-Life Stories

Story 1: Missing Good Acceptance Criteria

One of the most critical parts of a User Story is the acceptance criteria. It is the way the developer, Product Owner, and QA ensure they are on the same page. It is the place to think about all the scenarios to cover how the functionality will work. Only when all the acceptance criteria can be demonstrated to the Product Owner, and the Product Owner accepts the work, can the User Story be closed. So having people who can write good acceptance criteria is important. I was on one Scrum team that wrote acceptance criteria using the BDD given-when-then format. We would then take the acceptance criteria and use them to create JBehave story files. Over time we realized this was not a good practice, but I will talk about that in Story 2. Rather, the issue I saw on this team was the fact that the SDET on the team was writing the acceptance criteria. This seemed odd to me from the start and when I asked why it was being done this way, nobody seemed to have a good answer. The logic was that the SDET is doing the testing, so why not have him write the acceptance criteria as well? This did not work well on this team or other teams that I have seen. I think the reason is that being a good SDET or QA engineer is not the same as knowing the business domain and being able to think through all the scenarios for a given User Story. The acceptance criteria were not very clear and things were missed. This hurt both the quality of the software and the team's velocity.

Thoughts

It is not that a SDET or automation engineer cannot write good acceptance criteria, but rather I think it is just a different skill set. On teams where I've seen really thorough and well-written acceptance criteria, they were written by either a QA engineer or BA. They have a much better understanding, at least at the time the acceptance criteria are written, of what the User Story is about. From my experience, they are better suited to think through all the scenarios and articulate those in the acceptance criteria. The other point is that acceptance criteria should be a collaborative effort, not just a person handing off the acceptance criteria to a developer.

From my perspective, the order of testing scenarios goes something like this: acceptance criteria scenarios are first derived from business rules, and then automated tests are derived from the acceptance criteria scenarios. In terms of the format of the acceptance criteria, it does not have to be in the given-when-then format. In fact, I am a fan of using an example table, which I think can more clearly illustrate what the expected behavior should be. There are a lot of examples you can find on this approach, but I would recommend having a look at *Specification by Example* by Gojko Adzic (Manning Books, 2011).

Story 2: Great Collaboration

In contrast to the situation in Story 1, I was fortunate to be on an Agile project where the process for writing User Stories worked very well. On this particular project we had a process where the QA engineer would write the acceptance criteria for the User Stories. The QA engineer worked very closely with the Product Owner to get answers and to make sure they understood all the scenarios for the User Story.

When a developer was ready to start working on a User Story, he or she would meet with the QA engineer to discuss the story. They would review the typical "as a blank, I want to be able to blank, so that I can blank," and then they would review all the acceptance criteria. There would be some back and forth about whether the scenarios were clear enough or maybe some scenarios were not covered. The result of this meeting, which could be as short as ten minutes, is that the developer and the QA engineer were on the same page about the User Story. This does not mean things can't change, but at least we were on the same page before development started and we worked together to obtain a shared understanding of the work that needed to be done.

Once everyone was on the same page in terms of what it meant to be "done done" for the User Story, on this particular team the developers would take the acceptance criteria and convert them into automated functional tests using JBehave. When we gave the story to our QA engineer for testing, one of the things he would check is that the automated functional tests were written and matched what the acceptance criteria said. The QA engineer also ensured that the tests were passing in the CI pipeline.

Thoughts

In Agile software development, collaboration is critical, though I am a fan of process, because it helps with consistency and it helps with building a cadence. But to be clear, in Story 2 the team did not have hard and fast rules about when the developer would meet with the QA engineer and no formal meetings. Everyone on the team worked well together, and I could just walk over to the desk of one of the QA engineers and say, "Do you have a minute to discuss the User Story about X?" Of course, the QA engineer would not be completely surprised because in the Daily Stand-up I would have mentioned that chances were good that I would be starting on the next User Story in the backlog. Even if it was an unplanned meeting, it was never a big deal.

In the case where, perhaps, the scenarios were not complete, the developer would offer to help make the changes. This allowed the developer to help unblock the User Story and hence development could begin. This was probably one of the best examples of teamwork that I had ever seen on a project.

Story 3: Quality of Test Code

While I was a member on one Scrum team I saw how managers who are not technical can make decisions that really hurt code quality. On this particular Agile project we were using JBehave to write our BDD tests. JBehave is a BDD framework written in Java. The manager of my team thought that any developer could write the automated functional tests using JBehave, so our web developers started writing the automated functional tests. It is not that this is necessarily a bad thing, except in this instance our web developers did not have experience writing Java code. It was great that the web developers were getting a chance to learn Java. However, our team said that we wanted to treat our automated functional tests as production-quality code. So in that sense I didn't think it was a good idea to have people brand new to Java writing code that should be production-quality code. By the end of the project we had a significant amount of Java code that was not that well written and had to be refactored.

Thoughts

In Story 3, the main issue was that the manager was so determined to prove his theory that all developers have the same abilities that he was willing to hurt the team's velocity and put the quality of the software at risk. I even discussed this with the manager at one point, saying that all developers don't have the same skill sets and that expecting someone new to writing Java code to produce the same quality of code as someone who has been writing Java code for years was not reasonable.

The main point is that I think test code, both unit and functional, should be the same quality as production code. No less emphasis should be placed on this code. Only when you have quality test code can you have confidence in your application and only then can you really think about CD. If you do not have high confidence that you have not broken anything in the application, then you would need to rely on a lot of manual testing, and that is just not feasible for most applications.

Story 4: Too Many Sources of Truth

One thing that plagues many teams is how to document requirements and how to make sure that they reflect what the code actually does. I've seen this on a lot of Agile projects. On one project we had documentation of requirements, functional tests, and the actual code for the tests all in different places. We kept the acceptance criteria on wiki pages. We had the definition of the functional tests in text files. Finally, we had the code for the functional tests in source control. Not surprisingly, these became quickly out of sync. Our team could not trust the wiki pages or the text files. The only way to truly know how the application was working was to look at the actual code for the functional tests (in this case it was Java).

By the end of this project we had hundreds of User Stories on the wiki that people could not trust, and they were essentially thrown away. So, instead of updating the existing User Story and its acceptance criteria whenever we added new functionality, we created brand-new User Stories and acceptance criteria. It was like starting from scratch for each new project. Then, at the end of the next project, we again could not trust the wiki pages and they again became outdated. This was such a terrible waste of time and effort, and at the end we had nothing, except the code for the functional tests, that actually told us what the application was doing.

Thoughts

A better approach, in my opinion, is to have "living documentation" that evolves over time and gives you the confidence that the application is behaving the way you think it should. So, how do we go about getting living documentation? What does it really mean? A good place to start is by looking at some of the articles by Gojko Adzic. There are other great articles out there as well.

Essentially, the goal is to have documentation that is a living, breathing thing that evolves over time. It should be something that can be executed every time code is checked in to source control. In other words, as part of CI you would run these tests and if they passed, you would know that the application was behaving as expected. There are several approaches to accomplish this goal. You can use things like Cucumber or JBehave. Basically, you are putting the acceptance criteria from the User Story into these frameworks and running them on every commit of code. When you add new features or the behavior of the application is changed, you update these files so that the new version is run when developers check in code. In this way, the documentation is truly "living" and changes over time.

This living documentation becomes the "source of truth" and is the one place everyone can look to understand how the application works. For example, in an e-commerce application, I could look at the story file (if I were using something like JBehave) for adding items to a cart to understand how this works in the application. If this set of acceptance criteria (i.e., the story file in JBehave) is passing in CI, then I know the application is doing what I expect. Better yet, anyone can look at these acceptance criteria and can understand what the system is doing. In other words, the acceptance criteria are in the BDD language using the given-when-then structure. This means Product Owners, QA engineers, and developers are all looking in one place to understand how we expect the application to work. It means no more having multiple sources of truth (i.e., wiki pages, text files in source control, and maybe even some spreadsheets somewhere).

The framework you use, how you integrate this approach into your current CI pipeline, and how you fit this into your overall Agile development will obviously vary from team to team. But I think the benefits of using living documentation are worth at least trying to see if it will work for your team and organization. I think the time saved, reduction of redundant documentation, single source of truth, and increased confidence that what is coming out of your CI pipeline actually works the way you think it should are all reasons for considering using some sort of living documentation.

Story 5: One Size Does Not Fit All

When it comes to testing software, each company seems to do things a little differently. In some companies you have a central group of people who do manual testing. In other companies you have QA engineers as part of a Scrum team. In other companies you have business users who test the software. Regardless of whether or not a company is using Agile software development, I've seen that what works for one company does not necessarily work for another company. I've seen this in several companies that try to adopt what the "cool kids" are doing. The best example of this occurred when a QA director introduced many concepts that he read about that were working for companies that are "software giants."

This director introduced two changes: a centralized QA group and adding a SDET to each Scrum team. Previous to these changes, we had a QA engineer on each cross-functional Scrum team. The main problem was that there was a lack of understanding of how the existing Scrum teams in this organization functioned. The changes were introduced completely based on what was working for other companies. The problem was that this particular company did not have the same culture, infrastructure, or way of working as these "software giants." The changes were introduced without understanding how Agile was working in this company and the importance of having a cross-functional Scrum team.

When these changes were implemented, the embedded QA engineers were removed from the Scrum teams and a SDET was added to the team. But the SDET role in this company was very different from what it was at other companies. These changes led to a less knowledgeable central QA group because now the group was not involved in the development of the features. Testing became slower, many areas were not covered, and defects were not detected. In general, the quality of the application suffered. This was due in part to the lack of automated tests. It also created a classic "throw it over the wall" mentality. So once teams finished their Sprints and collected their points, they were really not concerned about what testing would happen later.

Thoughts

I'm definitely an advocate of trying new things, as I've mentioned in other chapters in this book. But there are some critical components that need to be in place. For example, there needs to be a culture of openness so people can speak up when something is not working. Then, of course, these concerns need to be heard and acted on by people who have the power to change things.

Following are some of the things to look out for and how to fix things:

First, look at your culture. Just because some process works at some other company does not mean it will work at yours. Each company, and even organization, has its own culture. Will introducing something like centralized QA work in yours?

Second, don't set things in stone. One of the issues with the situation in Story 5 is that it was approached as a mandate and it was absolute.

Third, listen to your teams. When everyone from managers to developers starts complaining that things have been made harder and that the software quality is impacted, those concerns should probably be heard.

Finally, let the numbers tell the story. If after a big change you see the defect counts go up, testing takes twice the amount of time, or releases are always late, then you need to take a close look to see if problems these are a result of the change. If they are a result of the change, then be open to rolling back the changes or adjusting the areas that are harming software development.

Story 6: Worth the Investment

In my opinion, automated functional testing is one of the best investments a team can make. It can help catch defects before they get to Production and give you confidence that the application is still working the way you expect it to. But you need to invest in the right tests and environments to run the tests. I was on one team that was adopting Agile and the team made a good start by creating a few automated test scripts. The team was using Selenium Grid to run the tests. We had a small test suite for this particular e-commerce web site. For every release we would run the tests to make sure that nothing was broken. This was a great start since previously we had had no automated tests. In this particular case the test scripts were run against the web site once it was pushed to the Production environment (i.e., was live to anyone who hit the web site). The test scripts, since they were running in Production, did not go through the checkout process because that would have created real orders; creating real orders would decrement inventory for real customers, so that would not have been good).

Thoughts

If you don't currently have automated test scripts, then you are missing out on an opportunity to increase quality and reduce manual testing. So adding any tests, even if they point to a Production version of your web site, is better than nothing. But, as mentioned in Story 6, that should just be a starting point.

Ideally, you run the automated functional tests before you deploy the code to a Production environment. Perhaps this is not an option in your particular case, so running against Production might be something you just have to live with and you might be limited in what you can test in an automated fashion. But if you can create a test environment (usually a Stage or Preview environment) and run the tests against that environment, then that is preferred.

The other issue in Story 6, again because the team was limited to running against Production, was that the automated functional tests did not test one of the most critical parts of the web site: the checking out of the cart. In this particular case I asked the QA engineer if he was testing that part of the web site manually, and he said "no." I was a bit surprised and the reason he gave was that no one wanted to use a personal credit card. I recommended to our manager we get a corporate card that the QA engineer could use to test the checkout process every time we pushed a release to Production. Again, this is not ideal by any means, but if you can automate testing 75% of your web site and then manually test the remaining areas (especially the critical areas like checking out a cart), then that is a great improvement over not having any automated testing.

One technique I've used with good success is the concept of developing "User Journeys." Basically, you create a set of personas and then walk through how that persona would interact with your web site. After you have these User Journeys, you can automate parts of them and build on that automation over time. Of course, the User Journeys themselves will evolve over time. So, for example, if you had an Online Travel site, one persona might be "Susan, a mother of three planning vacation for her family." Then you develop a User Journey for this persona, like "Susan wants to explore hotels around the Orlando area" and "She wants to be able to sort by price" and "Once she finds a hotel she will add it to her cart and check out." This allows you to understand, at a high level, how real users might interact with your web site. Once you have some User Journeys, you can automate the most critical parts, like adding items to a cart or checking out. There are many great articles on User Journeys, and I would recommend doing more research if you are interested in learning a different way to look at how to test your web site.

The idea of automated test scripts is not specific to Agile by any means. However, I think when adopting Agile software development methodology, automated functional testing becomes even more important because of things like CD and BDD. In order to release software often, it is critical that you have a high level of testing, and typically this testing needs to be automated because manual testing simply takes too long and does not catch everything.

Some Process Required

Although the flavors of Agile vary on their level of prescriptiveness, it doesn't mean that you can't still have other processes in place that add value. I've lost count of how many times I've heard "we're Agile" when a team doesn't want to adopt any rules or process. If you ask about documentation, or lack thereof, they say "we're Agile." If you ask about the mountain of technical debt, they say "we're Agile." If you ask about design, they say "we're Agile." The point is that beyond the roles, meetings, and methods that each flavor of Agile prescribes, there is a need for other processes to ensure that quality software is being delivered. The counterargument is that having any kind of process is "anti-Agile" in some way, but that simply is a misunderstanding of Agile software development.

Real-Life Stories

Story 1: Process Can Add Value

Having been on several large Agile projects I've seen the difference that having good processes can make. On one project, for example, we had a process for code reviews. Since there were many developers all in the same codebase, it was critical that all the code adhere to our architectural and quality guidelines. To help ensure this was happening, we had approved code reviewers who were responsible for completing each code review. This process had the potential of creating a bottleneck, but for the most part, it worked very well. On another project there was no such process and the code quality was much lower.

Another example occurred on one project where we had a well-defined task workflow. We were using a physical task board, but it would have worked with an issue tracking system as well. For example, as part of our workflow we defined what should happen when a defect is raised in the Sprint demo. This meant that the entire cross-functional team was on the same page. The QA engineer knew who to assign the defect to and to mark the User Story as blocked. The developer knew to fix the defect before starting on any new User Story.

Thoughts

To have processes documented and followed by an Agile team is definitely not "anti-Agile." It is when your processes are so rigid and they are given more weight than the people and collaboration that you are then violating a core Agile principle. In fact, I think having good processes can actually support the Agile principles and help teams deliver valuable software faster. One of the ways it does this is by adding consistency and leveling expectations, which, in turn, makes teams faster because everyone is on the same page. In addition to putting good processes in place, in some organizations you don't have much of a choice but to follow defined processes. So, I think finding areas that can benefit from some defined process (perhaps go through a Value Stream Mapping exercise) and then creating and refining that process can really make a big difference for Agile teams.

Story 2: Clear Rules

There are many things outside Agile that teams have to deal with every Sprint. If you don't have processes in place to deal with these things, it can really hurt a team's velocity. While on one Agile project I saw this first-hand in the form of scope changes for User Stories. We would review the User Stories during Sprint Planning. As usual in Scrum, we would ask questions, re-estimate, and finally commit to a set of User Stories to fill the Sprint Backlog. But inescapably during the Sprint, requirements would change. On past projects we would absorb these changes. But on this project we decided to have a process in place to handle these changes. We would create a Change Request whenever the business would change the scope of a User Story and then the business would prioritize the change in the Product Backlog.

Thoughts

Story 2 provides a simple example, but having that process in place made a big difference. First, it took pressure off developers to absorb extra work. Second, we were able to keep our original point commitment (we were using Scrum). Third, it put the pressure on the business to write good User Stories. Finally, it made the collaboration between the Agile team and the Product Owner better because everyone was clear on how to handle scope change.

Story 3: Simple Definitions

When I've been a Scrum Master, I've typically preferred to keep the Scrum board as simple as possible. For example, I prefer to have just the basic states of "Not Started," "In Progress," "Being Tested," and "Done" on the board. But how does the team know when a User Story can make it into the Sprint Backlog in the first place? I was on one team where we had clear definitions of what "Ready for Development" meant and only when a User Story met all the criteria would it be brought into the Sprint Backlog. It was a checklist of sorts that we used during our Sprint Planning meeting. It did not replace the communication in the meeting but was, rather, a way to make sure we didn't forget anything that had bitten our team in the past. These criteria changed over time as the team learned more. It really helped to reduce the amount of times the team was blocked in the Sprint. I've also been on teams that did not have this process in place and from my experience those teams had a less predictable velocity.

Thoughts

The point of Story 3 is that you can complement Scrum with processes that work for your team. There is no right answer and each team is different. You need to do what works for you. Some of the processes and the "Ready for Development" checklist I mentioned came out of the team's Retrospective meetings. In this team's case, making the checklist part of our process made the team faster, which meant we could deliver more valuable software to the business.

Physical vs. Virtual

Agile software development talks a lot about communication and collaboration, and rightfully so. Communication and collaboration are a huge part of being successful with Agile: the collaboration between the team and the business; the communication between team members and Scrum Master. So, how can teams maximize collaboration and communication? How do things like distributed teams affect the ability to have great collaboration and communication? How does the use of physical and virtual tools affect this ability? Are there compromises that we simply must accept when it comes to having great collaboration and communication? I think the key is to find what works for your team and adjust often so that communication and collaboration are as effective as possible.

Real-Life Stories

Story 1: Physical Board Seems More Satisfying

I was on one Agile team that was lucky enough to be co-located. We had the Scrum team, Product Owner, and User Experience team all in one place. We started by using index cards for our User Stories, then transferred them to sticky notes and moved them to the task board. It was the typical Scrum board with the blue tape and everything. It worked really well for that team. Every day we would go into the conference room and go around the table to get an update from everyone. It was great to see subtasks and stories moving across the board every day. It was also nice that anyone could walk into the conference room and see exactly what the progress of the team was for the Sprint.

In addition to the physical Scrum board, we also used Jira to track issues. The reason for using something like Jira was to report to executives and for the Project Management group. So, even though it meant a little more work, we maintained both the physical and virtual task boards. For the most part, everyone on the team did a good job of keeping things up to date. The virtual board was synced every morning with the physical board after our Daily Stand-up meeting. Often the Scrum Master would do this synchronization task, which left developers free to get back to developing.

Thoughts

Having a physical Scrum board really worked for the Agile team in Story 1. I have been on several Scrum teams since then that used a physical Scrum board and have seen that it usually works really well for co-located teams. There is just something about moving a series of sticky notes across the board that feels good. It was also easy to see exactly how the Sprint was going just by looking at the board (i.e., it was obvious if the board was not changing every day). By the end of the Sprint seeing a bunch of sticky notes all moved to the "Done" column was a visual reminder of all the work the team had done during the Sprint.

Yes, you can track User Stories, subtasks, action items, and so on in a virtual tool like Jira, but I find it slower and it just doesn't have the same impact. Of course, you don't always have a; maybe your team is distributed or management mandates using something like Jira. Don't get me wrong, using something like Jira has many benefits that are very useful (reporting, trending, etc.). My recommendation would be, if you must use a virtual Agile tool, to also try to use a physical Scrum board and see if it helps the team.

Story 2: Combined Team Meetings

Distributed teams are common for many companies and organizations. For organizations doing Agile software development this can be a challenge. I've been on several Agile projects that had distributed teams. When I talk about distributed teams here, I am talking about Agile teams distributed on the same project. On one such an Agile project, two Scrum teams were working together out of the same Product Backlog.

The manager of the project decided that the two teams should have all Scrum meetings together. Although I don't agree with that approach, it might have worked on its own. However, in this case the two teams were in different locations. That compounded the issue because it made communication and collaboration much harder. We tried many techniques to help make communication and collaboration better. This included having a monitor set up all day with Skype so the two teams could see each other and ask questions through the day. We tried to always use VTC (video teleconferencing) for meetings so that it felt like the teams were together.

None of these things really made a difference. In some ways they made things worse. We spent the beginning of every meeting setting up whichever tool we were using to video conference. People dialed into meetings would get lost as soon as there were side conversations (there always seemed to be side conversations). The Daily Stand-up meeting was a good example. Sometimes we would just dial into a conference bridge and it seemed like we were just going through the motions and not getting the real value that the Daily Stand-up is supposed to provide.

Thoughts

As I mentioned, I think that having Scrum teams share the Scrum meetings is actually a bad practice. I think it is fine to have teams work from the same Product Backlog, but I think it is better to maintain separate teams and meetings. Beyond that, when the teams are not co-located, I think it is even worse to share meetings. Technology can only help so much with distributed teams. When you are spending half the meeting setting up and sharing documents, and so on, does that really add value?

If you are lucky enough to have members of a team co-located but perhaps the Product Owner is in a different location, then I think it is better to have separate meetings for each Scrum team. The Product Owner can attend the meetings for each team (Sprint Planning, etc.). If there is a concern that the teams will not know what the other is doing (specifically when they are working from the same Product Backlog), that is where a "Scrum of Scrums"-type meeting can provide some value.

The main point I'm trying to make in regard to Story 2 is that sometimes we lose sight of what adds real value (i.e., communication and collaboration) when we try to use tools to compensate for teams not being co-located. If you see this happening, it is time to re-evaluate how your team is working and raise red flags in the team's Retrospective meeting.

Final Thoughts

One of the primary reasons for writing this book was to share my experiences from over six years on Agile projects and, ideally, to help other development teams learn from others' mistakes. I'm a big believer in learning from others' experience and not repeating the mistakes and going through the same pain. On several Agile projects, I've see new teams refuse to ask more seasoned teams for advice. Perhaps they just wanted to learn on their own and not be influenced by others' experiences. Maybe they thought they had all the knowledge and tools they needed to be successful. But, inevitably, I would hear them go through all the same pain that other teams had gone through and long since learned from. That's why I wanted to share these stories. Not every team is the same and not every scenario is covered here; that could never be the case. There is no right answer and the thoughts about each story are just my opinions and based on what I have personally experienced.

Even if you read through the stories and don't agree with my views, I hope this book has made you rethink some of the things your organization is doing and has given you some ideas of things to try. It is not meant to be a step-by-step guide. Ask any Agile Coach how many times he or she has been asked, "Are we doing Agile right?" Everyone wants to know "the steps to doing Agile the right way" and wants a clear set of steps and tools that will make them "Agile." I know I was guilty of wanting such a clear and concise answer when I first starting using Agile. But what you learn along the way is that it is not about process or tools; rather, Agile is a way of developing and delivering software. It's about values and a set of principles that guide the way you develop and deliver software. These values and principles are rooted in the Agile manifesto and how you achieve them will be different for every team.

There is no single value or principle to focus on, but I think some are more critical than others. If I had to focus on three areas more than any other they would be collaborating, morale, and testing.

The importance of collaboration cannot be overstated. Having great team-work on the Agile team and open communication with the Product Owner are vital. If everyone on the team knows what is the others are doing, then people can share ideas, reduce duplication of effort, and swarm to keep every-one moving forward. Having open communication with the Product Owner (or business in the more general sense) is also key. It means you are being transparent and that allows the Product Owner to prioritize work. It also means the Product Owner knows exactly what the team is doing and there shouldn't be any surprises at the end of each Sprint.

Whether you are using Agile or not, morale is always important. But when using Agile software development I would say it is more important, or at least changes in morale are more visible. On a Scrum team, for example, when the morale of the team is poor, velocity usually suffers. Velocity can suffer because of more defects being introduced. Hence more time is spent on defects and less time is spent on User Stories. Of course, negative morale is never a good thing and can have more effects beyond the Scrum team. I've seen some really amusing things done to developers that killed morale: everything from one manager giving us three-day-old donuts as a reward to an executive stating that developers wanted to work late so they could get free pizza. Of course, these are minor things, if not funny in hindsight, but the point is that things like this can hurt morale. One thing I've done on some Scrum teams was to have a "Sprint rock star" award. The team would vote anonymously every Sprint for the person who should get the award. It really helped to keep morale high and show that people on the team were appreciated.

A lot of organizations talk about how they are "Agile" because they have set up CI. While CI is a first step, it is often not the last step in being able to deliver quality software. Unit testing is critical and a must for CI to have any value. But if teams want to have a high level of confidence that what comes out of the CI pipeline is potentially shippable, then a serious investment in testing is required. Without automated tests, it means a lot of manual testing and very low confidence that the software is working as expected. Unit tests are one part of automated testing, from a CI pipeline standpoint, but functional tests are also important. Just because unit tests pass, that does not mean your application is behaving as expected. That is where BDD comes into the picture. I am a big believer in BDD and the value that it provides an Agile team. With good unit tests and functional tests, a team will have much higher confidence when everything passes that the software is working as expected. But creating automated functional tests and maintaining them takes a lot of investment. I've been on several Agile projects whose leaders were not willing to make this investment and paid the price for years in terms of high defect counts and bad user experiences. I'm not talking about writing a functional test for every feature that is developed, but you start with the most critical aspects of your application and then add tests as you find troublesome areas.

BDD, CD, and automated functional testing are all important areas to think about. Each is a big topic on its own, but I believe it is critical for an Agile team to understand these topics and see how they can improve software quality, time to market, and overall confidence in the software that the team is delivering to the business.

References

Adzic, Gojko. (2011, June 6). *Specification by Example: How Successful Teams Deliver the Right Software*. Shelter Island, NY: Manning Books.

Fowler, Martin. (2010, October 29). FeatureToggle [bliki]. Retrieved from `http://martinfowler.com/bliki/FeatureToggle.html`.

Humble, Jez and David Farley. (2011). *Continuous Delivery: Reliable Software Releases Through Build, Test, and Deployment Automation*. New York: Pearson Education.

West, Dave. (2011, December 15). Analyst Watch: Water-Scrum-fall is the reality of agile. Retrieved from `http://sdtimes.com/analyst-watch-water-scrum-fall-is-the-reality-of-agile/`.

Index

U

Unity building
    aforementioned items, 49
    Agile Coach/CSM, 46
    building team morale, 48
    building working software, 43
    collaboration, 47
    communication, 43
    cross-functional team, 47
    CSMs, 46
    learning, 46
    management, 48
    members of team, 47
    peer pressure, 44
    point commitment, 45
    Sprint commitment, 43–45
    teamwork, 47

V

Value people over process, 16
Velocity plan, 30
Video teleconferencing (VTC), 89

W, X, Y, Z

Water-Scrum-fall, 37
Work-In-Progress (WIP), 35
Work-life balance, 33
    cadence creation, 34–35
    cross-functional team, 35
    death marches, 36
    high-priority defects, 36
    management's support, 36
    mandating velocity, 33–34

Get the eBook for only $5!

Why limit yourself?

Now you can take the weightless companion with you wherever you go and access your content on your PC, phone, tablet, or reader.

Since you've purchased this print book, we're happy to offer you the eBook in all 3 formats for just $5.

Convenient and fully searchable, the PDF version enables you to easily find and copy code—or perform examples by quickly toggling between instructions and applications. The MOBI format is ideal for your Kindle, while the ePUB can be utilized on a variety of mobile devices.

To learn more, go to www.apress.com/companion or contact support@apress.com.

Apress®
THE EXPERT'S VOICE™

Printed in the United States
By Bookmasters